*A tragedy of Cola's furie*

# A TRAGEDY

OF

# COLA'S

# FVRIE

OR

# LIRENDA'S

## MISERIE

Written by Henry Burkhead, 1645.

Printed at
KILKENNY,
1645.

And are to be sold at the signe of the white
Swanne, in Kilkenny. M. DC. XLVII.

# A TRAGEDY OF COLA'S FURIE, OR LIRENDA'S MISERIE

by Henry Burkhead

*edited by*
Angelina Lynch

*with an introductory essay by*
Patricia Coughlan

FOUR COURTS PRESS

Set in 10.5 pt on 13 pt Bembo for
FOUR COURTS PRESS LTD
7 Malpas Street, Dublin 8, Ireland
e-mail: info@fourcourtspress.ie
http://www.fourcourtspress.ie
*and in North America for*
FOUR COURTS PRESS
c/o ISBS, 920 N.E. 58th Avenue, Suite 300, Portland, OR 97213.

A catalogue record for this title
is available from the British Library.

ISBN 978-1-84682-108-0

This book is published in an edition of 300 copies
of which 250 are for sale.

Printed in England
by CPI Antony Rowe, Chippenham, Wilts

# Contents

# The Literature of Early Modern Ireland series

*Previously published in the series:*
Faithful Teate's *Ter Tria* ed. Angelina Lynch (2007)

*Forthcoming volumes in the series:*
Richard Nugent's *Cynthia* (1604) ed. Angelina Lynch, with an introduction by
    Anne Fogarty
William Dunkin's *The Parson's Revels* (*c.*1745) ed. and introduced by Katie Skeen
The anonymous 'Purgatorium Hibernicum' (1668–70) ed. Andrew Carpenter
    and Nicholas Williams
Henry Burnell's *Landgartha* ed. Deana Rankin

# Preface

This series of editions of English-language texts from seventeenth- and eighteenth-century Ireland has been undertaken in the belief that the study of Early Modern Ireland is in a new and exciting phase. As thousands of web-based images of English-language texts from Early Modern Ireland have become available to scholars and students during the last few years (through 'Early English Books Online' and the 'Eighteenth Century Collections Online' for instance), so the necessity for authoritative editions of key texts has become ever more acute. Interest in Early Modern Ireland is constantly increasing and what is needed now is a series of definitive editions of some key literary and dramatic texts, edited to the highest standards and set into context by scholars and editors of international standing: such is this series.

The series was originally conceived as one which would embrace verse and drama before embarking on the rather more substantial prose texts of the period. However recent developments have led to a very welcome arrangement by which a series of prose fictions (*c*.1680–*c*.1820), under the editorship of Professor Ian Campbell Ross of Trinity College Dublin, Dr Aileen Douglas of Trinity College Dublin and Dr Moyra Haslett of Queen's University Belfast, will appear alongside the verse and drama texts originally envisaged.

Meanwhile, our particular thanks go to Dr Angelina Lynch who has worked enthusiastically and tirelessly on the editorial side of this project for the last two years. Her energy and commitment have been exemplary – and we are particularly fortunate that she was prepared to risk eyesight and sanity in transcribing *Cola's Furie* from the extraordinarily difficult (sometimes almost unreadable and often only barely intelligible) unique copy of the text. We are all in her debt.

Andrew Carpenter
General Editor
Dublin, August 2008

# Acknowledgments

We are very grateful to Professor Patricia Coughlan for providing the introduction and appendix for this book.

The editorial work for this volume could not have been brought to completion without the award of an IRCHSS (Irish Research Council for the Humanities and Social Sciences) post-doctoral fellowship to Dr Angelina Lynch. We are grateful to the Council for its support of this project and to the UCD School of English, Drama and Film for hosting Dr Lynch during her fellowship.

We also acknowledge with thanks a grant to aid towards the costs of publication from the National University of Ireland.

Thanks are due also to Professors Danielle Clarke and Alan Fletcher of the UCD School of English, Drama and Film, to Dr Stephen O'Neill of NUI Maynooth and to the staff of the libraries of University College Dublin, Trinity College Dublin, the National Library of Ireland, the British Library and the Huntington Library, San Marino, California. Michael Adams, Martin Fanning and the team at Four Courts Press have been supportive and helpful in bringing the book into existence.

Angelina Lynch would also like to thank Andrew Carpenter for his support and encouragement.

# Introduction[1]

## Patricia Coughlan

For painfully obvious reasons, relatively few literary texts in English emerged in Ireland during the middle decades of the seventeenth century. Among these, *A tragedy of Cola's furie, or, Lirenda's miserie* (Kilkenny, 1646), a five-act verse tragedy or tragicomedy, is remarkable in several respects. Strongly taking the viewpoint of Catholics in the period, it draws capably on the tradition and conventions of contemporary theatre, and offers a vivid and disturbing experience, historically, emotionally and aesthetically.[2] There seems to be only one surviving copy, in the British Library.[3] It offers fascinating challenges which should prompt further investigation. Its reprinting in the present series, as part of the larger enterprise of enabling a more complete and coherent understanding of seventeenth-century Ireland and its writings, will make it far more readily available to all students both of theatre and of early modern Ireland. It holds considerable interest, not only for such scholars and not purely within the

---

1 This Introduction revises and updates my two previous essays: '"The modell of its sad afflictions": Henry Burkhead's *Tragedy of Cola's furie, or Lirenda's miserie*', in Micheál Ó Siochrú (ed.), *Kingdoms in crisis: Ireland in the 1640s* (Dublin, 2001), pp 192–211, and '"Enter Revenge": Henry Burkhead and *Cola's furie*', *Theatre Research International*, 15:1 (1990), 1–17. Material from these two essays has been reprinted with permission from Four Courts Press and Cambridge University Press.

2 It was noticed in A. Harbage, *Annals of English drama, 975–1700* (revised by S. Schoenbaum, London, 1964), in C. Langbaine, *Outline of the English dramatic poets* (Oxford, 1691), pp 41–2, in G.E. Bentley, *The Jacobean and Caroline stage*, iii (Oxford, 1956), 94–5, and briefly discussed in Christopher Morash, *A history of Irish theatre, 1601–2000* (Cambridge, 2002), pp 10–12. Longer discussions appeared in La Tourette Stockwell, 'Lirenda's Miserie', *Dublin Magazine* n.s., v (1930), 19–26, (largely however, a plot summary); Peter Kavanagh, *The Irish theatre* (Tralee, 1946), intemperately negative; and, more productively, G.C. Duggan, *The stage Irishman* (Dublin, 1937), pp 65–73. Dale B.J. Randall explored *Cola's furie* in the context of literary history in *Winter fruit: English drama, 1642–1660* (Lexington, 1995), pp 88–92, and John Kerrigan has recently added a substantial discussion which helps illuminate the larger political and ideological contexts, in *Archipelagic English: literature, history, and politics, 1603–1707* (Oxford, 2008), pp 182–8.

3 BL C.2 1.c.54, which has a small number of MS annotations of unknown date, by way of historical identifications of the characters, alongside some of the 'Names of the Chiefe Actors'. These are tantalizingly faint and have also been half trimmed off.

Irish context, but for all those concerned with theatre history and historical practice, and with early modern literature in English.

After a brief summary account of *Cola's furie,* this Introduction discusses it
under five headings: I: contemporary critical approaches to early modern political drama; II: historical, political and military contexts; III: authorship, commendatory verses, language, date and printing; IV: the question of performance,
audience and theatre contexts in Ireland; V: Aesthetics and politics: *Cola's furie*
as literature. An Appendix discusses the historical identifications of the play's
characters to date.

*Cola's furie,* which is apparently the work of one Henry Burkhead (see
below, section III), emerges from a sophisticated political context in 1640s confederation Kilkenny; more generally, it comes out of the centuries'-old civic and
legal culture of the Old English, which had recently reached a high point in
1630s Dublin. The play's action, however, focuses on military combat and other
violent acts during the wars following the 1641 Rebellion. It is written mainly
in uncertain, often rather approximate, blank verse (that is, unrhymed iambic
pentameter, the flexible and spacious poetic instrument which is the principal
medium of classic English texts including Shakespeare's plays, *Paradise Lost,* and
Wordsworth's *Prelude*). The pentameter speeches and dialogue are occasionally
interspersed with passages of rhyme and with songs. Between the bouts of fighting there are two torture scenes, an episode of attempted rape, songs – some
courtly, one 'low' and performed by common soldiers – dances and two scenes
involving supernatural intervention, one by a set of classical divinities, one by
the figure of Revenge.

## I: CONTEMPORARY CRITICAL APPROACHES TO
## EARLY MODERN POLITICAL DRAMA

Theatre historians in the past tended to take a dismissive attitude to *Cola's furie,*
considering it no more than a slightly versified political pamphlet. Bentley, for
instance, calls it 'a crude and diaphanously veiled account of Irish affairs', and
Peter Kavanagh, in *The Irish theatre,* is contemptuous:

> It does not surprise us that Burkhead did not succeed in getting it acted ...
> It is very vulgar and, above all, bloody ... The only merit *Cola's Furie* has
> is its sincerity ... It is a pity that Burkhead had not written his account of
> the Insurrection as chronicles ... As it is, *Cola's Furie* is worthless. (47–8)

Certainly the dramatic texture is loose, and *Cola's furie* passes from incident to
incident without a very strong sense of overall dramatic necessity, though with
lively alternations of sensation. The succession of events seems largely deter-

mined by that of history. However, this episodic structure works very effectively in re-enacting and revealing the lack of co-ordination and the inconclusiveness of the Irish 1640s wars themselves.[4] The play is thus a good deal more and other than a versified chronicle. It sets up and exploits a series of contrasts in tone and a sensational dramatic climax in the death of the villain, Cola, altering historical sequence in order to do so. Any attempt to match the *dramatis personae* to their historical originals, and the incidents represented to theirs (see the Appendix below for a detailed discussion of such attempts to date), has a curious effect on the reader's experience of the play. It greatly diminishes initial impressions of gratuitousness or sensationalism, and gives a lively sense of the frustration, fear and political passion of those living through the period.

One of Burkhead's purposes may have been, in part, to counter virulent Protestant atrocity literature about the 1641 massacres, which circulated from 1642 on and which had taken on a propaganda life of its own.[5] *Cola's furie* lays great stress on violence being committed by the more extreme Angolean (English) commanders and on the judicial torture of the characters Rufus and Cephalon; it personifies in the figure of Cola himself a savagely irrational appetite for murderous cruelty. It draws upon Senecan models of a quasi-absolute rage, which had influenced Elizabethan tragedies, to realize this figure – one among many elements of the play which may indicate that it draws upon popular theatre of the 1630s.[6]

Recent scholarly work on English drama from 1640 to 1660, in particular that of Martin Butler, Sue Wiseman and Janet Clare, has revealed the energetic life of 1640s English political theatre, much of it popular, and just as decisively engaged on one side or the other as is Burkhead's play. This critical work, in the context of New Historicist and cultural-materialist theory, has actively re-envisioned the traditions of tragedy and chronicle play and of early modern literature more generally, in the context of new intellectual and ideological interest in the violent and polarized politics of the English Revolution period and in its writing.[7] This growing knowledge and deeper understanding of the nature of Eng-

---

4  See John Lowe, 'Some aspects of the wars in Ireland, 1641–1649', *Irish Sword*, 4 (1959), 82–7, and Micheál Ó Siochrú, *Confederate Ireland, 1642–49* (Dublin, 1998), pp 33, 55.

5  A representative early example of these pamphlets is Henry Jones' *A Remonstrance* (London, 1642), which was devastatingly effective in hardening English opinion against the Irish Catholics. There is a large and contentious historical literature on this subject; a balanced modern account of the depositions taken from victims, on which the atrocity accounts are based, is Aidan Clarke's 'The 1641 depositions', in Peter Fox (ed.), *Treasures of the Library, Trinity College Dublin* (Dublin, 1986), pp 11–120.

6  Compare Martin Butler's comments about the often patriotic and political plays put on at the London popular theatres in the decade up to 1642 in his *Theatre and crisis, 1632–1642* (Cambridge, 1984), pp 181–93.

7  See Martin Butler, *Theatre and crisis, 1632–1642* (Cambridge, 1984), Sue Wiseman, *Drama and*

lish drama in this very disturbed period would indicate that *Cola's furie* is not unlike many works actually produced on stage in England during this decade.

It can now be more clearly understood that the negative opinions of earlier commentators stemmed from an inappropriate set of aesthetic expectations, developed from Victorian and Edwardian readings of Shakespearean tragedy severed from its context and that of subsequent decades. Accompanying aesthetic assumptions of a mutually oppositional relation between art and politics also blocked appreciation of dramatic writing which did not conform to any ideal of the well-made play. Changing approaches to the aesthetic-political nexus, and a far wider acquaintance with early modern theatre, have allowed us to see that Burkhead's play is no more 'crude' or 'vulgar' than much of the drama of its period in England. As has been pointed out by recent neo-Marxist critics, the political tensions and disruptions of the revolution and civil wars worked to fracture and dislocate, often productively, the smoothness of the drama's literary forms. Furthermore, Brechtian and existentialist reconceptions and practices in theatre and performance from the 1940s onwards have profoundly altered our appreciation of what can be accomplished on the stage.[8]

## II: HISTORICAL, POLITICAL AND MILITARY CONTEXTS

*Cola's furie* deals with the 1640s Irish wars which were initiated by the Irish Rebellion in autumn 1641. The action represents a military campaign which is fought by the opposing forces of Angola (England) and Lirenda (Ireland). It rehearses some crucial episodes in the wars which followed the 1641 Rebellion, concentrating on events which can be recognized as those of 1642 and 1643, ending with the proclamation of a 'cessation'. This was the first truce which was brokered in September 1643 by Ormond, the leading figure among Irish royalists, a member of the Butler family who had been at the head of the Hiberno-Norman élite for centuries, and a Protestant. Many prominent Catholics – 'Old English' or Gaelic Irish or of mixed ethnic origins – joined or attempted to take control of the revolt begun in October 1641 by the Ulster Irish. From this was born the confederation of Kilkenny, a formal assembly of Catholics which sat in the south-eastern city, home of the Ormond Butlers, from 1642 till 1648. The confederation had a considerable formal presence: it had an Assembly which

---

    *politics in the English Civil War* (Cambridge, 1998), and Janet Clare (ed.), *Drama of the English Republic, 1649–60* (Manchester, 2002). I thank all three, and my colleague James Knowles, for helpful discussion of *Cola's furie* and related issues.

8  See Catherine Belsey, *The subject of tragedy: identity and difference in renaissance drama* (London, 1985), and Jonathan Dollimore, *Radical tragedy* (Brighton, 1984), as well as Butler, *Theatre and crisis*.

replaced the Dublin Parliament as a gathering-place for the Catholic élite, and was the focus of considerable cultural sophistication, as well as political intrigue. In late 1645, as we shall see, the Papal Nuncio Rinuccini was received at Kilkenny with great pomp and ceremony.

To understand the political context of *Cola's furie*, it is necessary to understand that the complex web of connections and interdependencies in Stuart Ireland, especially among the élite, involved many cross-allegiances and tensions. For instance Ormond, the leading Protestant grandee of the period, who is represented as Osirus in the play, had a large number of natural supporters and close connections who found themselves among the confederates. These included his Catholic brother Richard Butler and his great-uncle Lord Mountgarret, president of the confederate Supreme Council. Significantly, Burkhead characterizes Osirus mostly as moderate, and he is explicitly exonerated from responsibility for the judicial torture of Catholics shown in the play.

The decision of Catholic lords and gentry to join the rising was partly triggered by the initially savage and repressive response of the Dublin lords justices. These were the Offaly planter William Parsons and John Borlase (Pitho and Berosus in the play). Their party was made up mainly of 'New English' – Protestants who had come to Ireland from Elizabethan and early Stuart England – and their descendants. Parsons had been one of those settlers early at the receiving end of the rebels' actions, and he had fled to England, where he was prominent in spreading the outraged response of the dispossessed English planters. Notable among the New English who took arms against the rebellion was Sir Charles Coote, a Co. Cavan settler and governor of Dublin, who figures (in a perverse sense, 'stars') in the play as Cola, the villain-protagonist. The New English in Ireland did not care about the ethnic origins of Catholics in Ireland, but furiously promised the eradication of all Catholics.[9] In the late autumn of 1641 and early in 1642 they ordered respected and elderly Old English gentlemen of the Pale, who patently had had nothing to do with the rising, to be racked in Dublin Castle.[10] This stance of the lords justices was echoed in the reaction to the rising of the English Parliament. In the first phase of the English Civil War (between king and Parliament) then on the point of breaking out, Parsons and Borlase were to become unequivocal Parliamentary supporters. From February 1642, Parliament instituted the series of monthly London Fast

---

9   See Richard Bellings, in John T. Gilbert (ed.), *History of the Irish Confederation and the War in Ireland, 1641–1649*, 7 vols (Dublin, 1882–91), i, 39–40.

10   Bellings gives the following account (in Gilbert, i, 78–9, 81–2) of the racking of Sir John Read (the character Rufus), represented in the play at iii, 139 and of its political effects: 'the torture Sir John Read suffered and the leading interrogatories put to him, while he lay on the racke, concerning the King's being privy to the raysing of the Rebellion, did compleat men's aversion to the State'. The aged Patrick Barnewall of Kilbrew, Burkhead's character Cephalon, was also tortured.

Sermons to invoke divine retribution on all Irish Catholics. Further, in March it passed the Adventurers' act, which promised to allot the lands of rebels to those making financial contributions to their reduction, and made no fine distinctions among Catholic landowners about culpability in the initial deeds of the rebellion. Another crucial factor in mobilizing members of the Catholic upper ranks, particularly in Leinster, producing what would become the confederate alliance, was a series of notorious brutalities practised by Coote at Clontarf, on the outskirts of Dublin, and in County Wicklow. The deeds of Parsons and Borlase and those of Coote, as we shall see, loom very large in the action of the play and find vivid representation there.

*Cola's furie* vividly rehearses the fears, anger and frustrations common to all Catholic members of the landed interest in Ireland. This consisted of a hereditary aristocracy and a gentry proud of its traditions of civility, in both of which Hiberno-Norman and native Irish ethnicities had become thoroughly mixed.[11] Supporting that interest and intimately bound up with it in the confederation, as I have noted, were the prosperous bourgeoisie, among whom we may undoubtedly count Henry Burkhead himself. Much in the manner of royalists in England at the time, the play repeatedly insists upon the mission of the Lirendeans (i.e. the Irish) to defend and rescue the king's prerogatives, which are under attack by 'an elected crew of shamelesse Roundheads' (i, 191: 'elected' is presumably a pun, invoking both the parliamentary and the Calvinist senses). Such protestations of loyalty to and defence of the king were, typically, said to have been made by the large band of rebels (mentioned earlier) who, according to her deposition, attacked Elizabeth Dowdall's house and stole her stock (TCD MS 829). The play uses sophisticated political language to defend the Catholic royalists in Ireland from the current imputation of automatic disloyalty to English rule, distinguishing *religious* allegiance to the Pope from *civil* allegiance to the king (i, 337–40). This position is close to what was perhaps the period's most eloquent constitutional statement of the political philosophy of the Catholic élite before the rebellion. This was the speech made by the gifted lawyer Patrick Darcy to the Irish Parliament in June 1641, which was subsequently printed for the confederation (Waterford, 1643): (Darcy has a minor part in the play as 'Dora'). The pamphlets of Nicholas French, bishop of Ferns, written in the

---

11 Micheál Ó Siochrú's *Confederate Ireland, 1642–1649* (Dublin, 1998) is the most comprehensive and illuminating discussion to date of the broad political background to *Cola's furie*; see also the earlier analyses by Patrick J. Corish, in 'The Rising of 1641 and the Catholic Confederacy, 1641–5', and 'Ormond, Rinuccini and the Confederates, 1645–9', in T.W. Moody et al. (eds), *A New History of Ireland*, iii (Oxford, 1976), 289–335. On the conflict of loyalties for the Catholic Anglo-Irish, see especially p. 312. D.F. Cregan's 'The Confederation of Kilkenny', (unpublished PhD thesis, National University of Ireland, 1947), is still useful; as is J.C. Beckett, 'The Confederation of Kilkenny reviewed', in M. Roberts (ed.), *Historical Studies*, ii (London, 1959), 29–41.

1660s but reflecting on the whole catastrophe of Catholic hopes in the Civil War period, are also of great interest as a retrospective account of the viewpoint from which *Cola's furie* is written.[12] The confederate 'model of government' drawn up in November 1642 was similar to the remonstrance of their grievances which the peace negotiators brought to Trim, Co. Meath in March 1643. This stressed the royal prerogative, castigated the intemperate actions of the lords justices, protested the legal penalties on Catholic practice, and appealed to the king above the heads of these mere officials of the executive.[13]

Contrary to previous interpretations asserting the polarizing role of ethnicity in the confederation, the historian Micheál Ó Siochrú has shown how important was the ethnic hybridity of the confederation as an alliance, expressing the intertwined backgrounds of many or most of the individuals who made it up. One of the most striking instances of this was the Assembly's rejection from the outset of any distinction between Irish or English, whether 'old' or 'new', 'upon pain of highest punishment' (October 1642).[14] *Cola's furie* implicitly reflects this position in consistently giving phrases such as 'my Countrey' to all the Catholic characters, and in referring to them collectively as 'Lirendeans'. Thus the play's first spokesmen for the Catholic cause, Athenio, expresses an 'ardent zeale/to right our natives slavery, and stop/ the current of their puritan designe/intended for our totall ruine' (i, 158–61).

Nevertheless Burkhead's representation is not quite free of ethnically partisan allegiance: he presents a misleading version of the historical facts in at least one instance. This is when he privileges the role of the relatively ineffectual general Preston (Abner), the confederate commander-in-chief who was ethnically Old English, over that of the brilliant Ulsterman Eoghan Rua Ó Néill (Owen Roe O'Neill: Theodorike in the play). Theodorike has a fairly prominent role – at the close of the second act of *Cola's furie,* he is given an eloquent elegiac speech about the sad fate of Lirenda – but there is no doubt that Abner is shown as the central Lirendean figure. So while Burkhead displays no particular hostility to the old Irish elements of the confederation, he shows natural leadership as residing with an Old English figure, however inadequate Preston's military leadership proved in the event. (This is a judgement of the type bitterly resented by the author of the polemical work *An aphorismical discovery of treasonable faction,* for whom O'Neill, descended from Gaelic chieftains, is the indisputable hero of the wars.)[15] Burkhead's omission also of the bitter personal rivalry which actually

---

12  *A narrative of the earl of Clarendon's settlement and sale of Ireland, The bleeding Iphigenia,* and *The unkind deserter of loyal men and true friends* (all Louvain, 1668, 1674, and 1676 respectively).

13  See the extensive discussions in Ó Siochrú, *Confederate Ireland,* pp 47ff. and 62–3.

14  Ó Siochrú, *Confederate Ireland,* p. 48.

15  An anonymous work collected in John T. Gilbert (ed.), *A contemporary history of affairs in Ireland from 1641 to 1652,* I, pt i (Dublin, 1879).

existed between Preston and O'Neill presumably follows from his desire both to downplay the role of the charismatic and gifted Northerner and to show Preston in the best possible light. Preston, a son of Lord Gormanston, was a member of one of the most important of Old English families in Ireland. Like many participants on the confederate side in these wars, he had gained experience and skills on the Continent in the Thirty Years War before arriving in Ireland in September 1642 from the Spanish Netherlands (iv, 1–39).

### III: AUTHORSHIP, COMMENDATORY VERSES, LANGUAGE, DATE AND PRINTING

Almost nothing is definitely known about Henry Burkhead, whose name appears in various forms and who has been mistakenly conflated with another similar-sounding writer.[16] Anthony à Wood rather slightingly calls Burkhead 'no Academian, only a Merchant of Bristol', and Langbaine's brief mention of *Cola's furie* repeats this description and says the play was never performed. A search of the Bristol city archives has failed to discover any mention of the author, which may indicate that he resided in Kilkenny and traded *with* Bristol. Neither have I been able to find him in educational records, and there seems at present no means of knowing how and where he acquired the degree of familiarity with the tradition, forms and conventions of English drama which underlie the play. Various forms of his surname do, however, occur in Bristol, and the name seems to be English, rather than an Irish one.[17] It is possible that he may have been among the recusants who had migrated from England in general and Bristol in particular in numbers, many settling in Waterford, in the decades before 1641.[18]

If we consider that he may not have been a first-generation settler, it is probably worth noting what is perhaps an outside chance: that he was a connection of

16  Wood is followed by Bentley in listing Burkhead as the author also of *The female rebellion* (*c*.1658), a political tragicomedy surviving in MS, and since identified as in fact the work of Henry Birkhead (1617?–1696). I thank Joan Pittock for kindly communicating to me her disentanglement of Burkhead from this Birkhead, Fellow of All Souls and founder of the Oxford Chair of Poetry, and also from his relative Sir John Birkenhead – the form in which W.S. Clark gives Burkhead's surname in *The early Irish stage* (Oxford, 1955), p. 40.

17  Joan Burkhead and Sarah and Thomas Burkett occur in *The inhabitants of Bristol*, in 1696, and Thomas Birket in the *City Chamberlain's Accounts*, in 1557. I am grateful for this information to Professor K.G. Davies; I also thank Mr John S. Williams of the Bristol Record Office, who searched that office's records for a mention of Henry Burkhead, without success.

18  Michael McCarthy-Morrogh, *The Munster Plantation: English migration to Southern Ireland, 1583–1641* (Oxford, 1986), pp 194, 210, 243, details this influx of English recusants and also an extensive human traffic to Bristol from Munster. I owe the references in this note and most of those following to David Edwards, who has generously shared his research on New English recusants in Ireland with me and whom I thank for several discussions about Burkhead's possible identity and background.

the prominent Co. Limerick family whose name is variously spelt 'Burgatt', 'Burgat', 'Burgett' or 'Burgate' (although to our ears the 'k' and hard 'g' sounds seem somewhat different). These Burgatts were also Catholics of New English origin. Forms of the name occur in the sixteenth century in Munster: a 'Thomas Burgate' was first Clerk of the Council to the Munster Presidency in 1570, then in 1576 Comptroller of Wine Imports at Cork. A 'John Byrket' (with a 'k'), possibly connected, was Attorney-General to the Munster Presidency in 1604.[19] Of the known Co. Limerick Burgetts, at least one seems to have been active in the 1641 rebellion. '[O]ne Burgett', described in a letter from the lords justices as 'commissary general of the rebells' army', was captured by Inchiquin early in September 1642 – therefore not long after the battle of Liscarroll – along with Colonel Richard Butler, 'son to the traitor the Lord Viscount Ikeryn'. These two escaped the fate of another fifty rebels caught at the same time, who were hanged next morning: this presumably indicates that, along with the nobleman's son, this Burgatt was considered to be of some social importance.[20] The role as commissary general – provider of supplies – is, of course, more than compatible with the occupation of merchant. A 'John Burgatt of neare Kilmallock' is named in the 1641 depositions: he was said to have been present, together with large numbers of other rebels including Purcells, O'Briens, Fitzgeralds, and a Butler, at the despoilment of Elizabeth Dowdall's house and possessions in Kilfinny, Co. Limerick during the rebellion. Further, a 'John Burgett', in this case described as 'Esquire', was said to have been with the rebels of Mountgarret's army at Lismore, Co. Waterford during the robbery of Daniel Spicer and the hanging of one Richard Magner. It is worth noting that on the latter occasion another alleged member of the rebels' group was Anthony Preston, who was a son of Sir Thomas Preston, general in the Catholic confederation and hero of *Cola's furie*.[21] Members of the Burgat(t) family had a strong clerical presence in seventeenth-century Munster: two were prominent Dominicans during the 'clandestine ministry' of the 1630s, and their family possessed the resources to donate silver chalices engraved with their name. One of these, a Henry, was prior of Kilmallock about 1639.[22] Finally, in 1661 the Capuchin and confederate historian Richard O'Ferrall wrote instructions from St Malo for a visit to Rome by the most eminent of these clerics, William Burgat, then Vicar-General of Emly and Procurator of the Province of Tuam. Friend of Oliver Plunkett, Burgat was eventually nominated archbishop of Cashel in 1669.[23]

19  James L.J. Hughes (ed.), *Patentee officers in Ireland, 1172–1826* (IMC, Dublin, 1960), pp 19, 21.

20  James Hogan (ed.), *Letters and papers relating to the Irish Rebellion*, IMC (Dublin, 1936), p. 149.

21  The Dowdall deposition (TCD MS 829), sworn in October 1642, and that by Spicer, sworn in August 1642, are quoted in Thomas Fitzpatrick, *Waterford during the Civil War (1641–1653)*, (Waterford, 1912), p. 58.

22  Thomas Flynn, *The Irish Dominicans, 1536–1641* (Dublin, 1993), p. 272.

23  J. Corish, 'Two contemporary historians of the confederation of Kilkenny', *IHS*, 8 (1953), 226;

About Burkhead himself, all that seems biographically certain is the inescapable inference from the play itself of his strong support of the Catholic cause. There is, however, no reason to doubt Langbaine's characterization of him as a merchant, and the role of many Catholic merchants in supporting the confederation is well known. Its Assembly usually met in the house of Richard Shee, a leading Kilkenny merchant and Mountgarret's nephew, and a number of wealthier merchants from several counties sat in the Assembly. While their social standing excluded them from the inner councils of the confederation, their professional services and those of others less eminent (such as Burkhead himself, perhaps) were much relied upon to provide vital financial resources.[24] Rinuccini's remark about the hapless Glamorgan after the failure of his mission in 1646 – that 'even the merchants had abandoned him' – is revealing as an indication that Glamorgan had not only run out of money or credit, but also apparently of credibility even among those of somewhat lower social status than the ruling classes.[25]

*Commendatory verses*

Providing a little help in placing the dramatist specifically in the south-eastern milieu, three sets of conventionally fulsome commendatory verses are printed with the play. These are by William Smyth, Paul Aylward, and Daniel Breede. I have not been able to throw any light upon Breede, but there are good candidates for the other two. William Smyth's verses, the shortest of the three sets, are dedicated 'To my loving and respected friend Mr Henry Burkhead Merchant, upon his Tragedie of COLA'S FURY.' This William Smyth may be the well-known figure who came from the West of England in 1630 and acted ably for the Butlers in many capacities: secretary, printer, and attorney.[26] He was rewarded in 1635 with a patent of arms and the gift of land at Damagh, Co. Kilkenny. There he founded a family whose members, though well-known and staunch Catholics, continued for decades to be closely associated with service to the Ormonds at home and abroad, thus making 'a successful marriage of political loyalty and reli-

Brendan Jennings, 'Miscellaneous documents III', *Arch.Hib.*, 15 (1950), 39, and the same author's *Micheál Ó Cléirigh* (Dublin and Cork, 1936), 210 n.16; Brendan Fitzpatrick, *Seventeenth-century Ireland: the war of religions* (Dublin, 1988), pp 233, 244.

24  Ó Siochrú, *Confederate Ireland*, pp 206, 216.

25  G. Aiazza (ed.), *The embassy in Ireland of Monsignor G.B. Rinuccini*, tr. Annie Hutton (Dublin, 1873), 167; quoted in John Lowe, 'The Glamorgan mission to Ireland, 1645–6', *Studia Hibernica* iv (1964), 192.

26  William Smyth was associated with several of the Butlers: he acted as highly trusted attorney, for example, on behalf of the Catholic Richard Butler of Kilcash in 1638 (NLI. MS 11,044 No. 99, Ormond Archives). For two other sets of verses by him, see Andrew Carpenter (ed.), *Verse in English from Tudor and Stuart Ireland*, (Cork, 2003) pp 273–5. See also Alan Fletcher, 'Select document: Ormond's civic entry into Kilkenny, 29–31 August 1646', *IHS*, 35:139 (May 2007), 365–79, which suggests he may have been the 'Mr Smith' who made a formal speech on this occasion.

gious deviation'.[27] This religious allegiance, together with William Smyth's own West of England origins, makes a link with Burkhead likely. Some of William Smyth's descendants were later dispossessed under the penal laws when a younger son became a Protestant and inherited the family property.[28]

Paul Aylward was probably a member of the prominent Clonmel and Waterford family of Catholic merchants. Major clients of the Ormonds at home, the Aylwards had an extensive trading presence and residence in continental European cities – Málaga, St Malo and Lisbon – during the later part of the century.[29] Those Catholic merchants who remained in Waterford were expelled during the Commonwealth; among these the best documented Aylward, John, who was to become grandfather of a duke of Norfolk, had an uncle named Paul who remained in Ireland. Among other things an attorney, this Paul Aylward was Deputy Clerk of the Staple in Waterford in 1640 and is also recorded as holding several prominent civic offices and functions there during the 1660s and early 1670s.[30]

*Language*

A linguistic peculiarity in the play is worth noting as an indication that Burkhead may have been born in Ireland. This is a construction, considered grammatically non-standard, which replaces the standard demonstrative adjective ('those') with a demonstrative pronoun ('them'): typical examples from the play include: 'them powers above'(i, 177), 'them pleasant smiles'(i, 386), and 'them gloomy shades' (iv, 84). I have counted a total of twelve instances of this idiosyncratic grammatical construction.[31] Further, there are two examples of the use of a singular verb following the plural subject which is qualified by 'them' in this sense, as follows: '*Them* Noble acts *renders*/you famous to posterity' (Berosus' speech, i, 86–

27  See *Transactions of the Kilkenny Archaeological Society*, i (1849–51), 260–3; Revd William Carrigan, *History and antiquities of the diocese of Ossory* (Dublin, 1905), iii, 442–5; Monica Brennan, 'Kilkenny landowners, 1641–1700', in William Nolan and Kevin Whelan (eds), *Kilkenny: History and Society* (Dublin, 1990), p. 117.

28  *JRSAI*, iii, n.s. (1860–1), 92.

29  Information from Julian Walton, 'The family of Aylward (Continued)', VI (a), *Irish Genealogist* 5:2 (1974), 218–19. I thank Julian for helpful discussions of the families of south-eastern Ireland.

30  'In 1661 and 1670 he was one of the clerks of the Lazarhouse or Leper Hospital; in 1664 he shared a house in Broad Street with Andrew Lynn and Thomas Strange; in 1671 he was admitted to be a Freeman of the City' (Walton, 218–19).

31  The others are: 'them looks of sadd dispaire' (i, 293), 'them who invoke your happy fates' (iii, 192; in this slightly different instance, 'them' is an incorrect form of the demonstrative pronoun), 'them grosse abuses' (iii, 330), 'them Christall streames' (iii, 350), 'them teares' (iii, 516), 'them lamps divine' (iv, 125), 'them adventures' (iv, 135), 'them true Emblems' (iv, 254–5)', them active veines' (v, 108), 'these drones, them viperous Locusts'(v, 379), and the two examples quoted in the text.

7; emphasis added). The other instance occurs in Tygranes' lines at iii, 505–7 (emphasis added):

> *Them* gentlemen
> that now are in restraint for the same fact
> *speakes* thy accomplisht willingnesse.

In both these cases the plural noun – 'acts' and 'gentlemen' respectively – would in standard English require a plural verb, i.e. 'render' and 'speak', and 'them' would be 'these' or 'those'. Some linguists, discussing twentieth-century usage, suggest that this construction – a singular verb after a plural subject, with 'them' – is typically Hiberno-English.[32] It is, of course, difficult to be sure either that this was so in the seventeenth century, or that it might not also characterize a West Country dialectal feature.

### Date and printing

One part of the play's prefatory material helps us to date it: Burkhead's dedication to the prominent English royalist Edward Somerset, who was sent in August 1645 as his envoy to the confederation by Charles I, then embroiled in civil war with Parliament and needing all the support, military and otherwise, he could get. Somerset was to be created earl of Glamorgan during 1646. This dedication employs the figleaf of a pretence that 'the subject of this small worke' is 'drawn from the historicall records of Forren countryes, and fitly applyable to the distempers of this Kingdome'. It compares Somerset to Noah's dove bringing the olive branch, praising his willingness

> with a glance of reall compassion to view and survey the modell of its sad afflictions, having with unspeakable toyle, charges, and dangers adventured hither … to appease the raging fury of our intestine harmes...[33]

It goes on to describe the play as

> these issues and ofsprings of a boyling & bleeding heart, boyling with impregnable love and loyaltie unto his Majestie, and bleeding for the continuall distempers of his Kingdomes.

---

32  For a full discussion of the morphology and syntax of seventeenth-century Hiberno-English, see Alan Bliss, *Spoken English in Ireland 1600–1740* (Dublin, 1979), pp 284–311. See also David Crystal, *Encyclopaedia of the English language* (Cambridge, 1995), p. 338. Crystal's example is 'Them cars is great'. I thank Elisabeth Okasha and Jeff Kallen for discussion of this.

33  This may refer not just to the general hazards of travel between Britain and Ireland (coasting Parliamentary vessels made communications difficult) but to the fact that Glamorgan was shipwrecked on his way to Ireland (Corish, 'The Rising of 1641 and the Catholic Confederacy, 1641–5', in Moody et al. (eds), *A new history of Ireland*, iii, 315).

Glamorgan, himself a Catholic, came to Dublin in July 1645 to try and ensure the speedy dispatch of Irish troops, desperately needed to help improve the position of the royalist army (decisively defeated at Naseby in June). The dedication helps to date the play because Somerset arrived in Kilkenny only in August 1645. Its narrative includes only events up to 1643, and the title page indicates that it was written and printed in 1645, but also 'to be sold at the signe of the white Swanne, in Kilkenny' in 1646. From this we may presume that it was written some time during the second half of 1645, although the dedication may, of course, have been appended only just before printing.

The other notable 1645 arrival in Kilkenny was that of Rinuccini, the papal legate to the confederation, in the autumn. *Cola's furie* has no Rinuccini figure, which may be indicative for the dating. Also the play does, of course, focus primarily on military events, in the tradition of heroic representations. But it is more likely to reveal a desire on Burkhead's part to play down papal involvement as taking from the confederates' professions of loyalty to the English monarch; this would clearly show that he himself did not belong to the 'clerical party' in the confederation.[34] This is further underlined by the fact that confederates who adhered to the Ormond peace, presented as the play's happy resolution, were censured by an Ecclesiastical Congregation at Waterford in August 1646.[35]

As for the printing of *Cola's furie*, it is not known whether the Jesuit press which then existed in the city was used, or that run by the confederate Supreme Council. If the latter, it is highly unusual in being a literary text amidst the political, religious and administrative documents, pamphlets and proclamations which make up the remainder of the output from Kilkenny.[36]

## IV: THE QUESTION OF PERFORMANCE, AUDIENCE, AND THEATRE CONTEXTS IN IRELAND

Langbaine and, as we have seen, Kavanagh, asserted that *Cola's furie* was meant purely as a closet drama and not for performance, though neither of them

---

34 See Kerrigan, 184–5 and Tadhg Ó hAnnracháin, *Catholic Reformation in Ireland: the mission of Rinuccini, 1645–1649* (Oxford, 2002).

35 Ó Siochrú (ed.), *Kingdoms in crisis*, p. 260.

36 See E.R. McClintock Dix, 'Printing in the city of Kilkenny in the seventeenth century', *Proceedings of the Royal Irish Academy*, 32 (1914), 125–37, and William Sessions, *The first printers in Waterford, Cork and Kilkenny pre-1700* (York, 1990), especially the comments by Derek Nutgall and James Mosley, 214, 279–1. *Cola's furie* is one of the earliest plays printed in Ireland. It was just preceded by Thomas Randolph's *Aristippus; or The jovial philosopher* (Dublin, 1635) and Henry Burnell's *Landgartha* (Dublin, 1641), a historical romance with an ostensibly Danish, but allegorically Irish, setting, performed in Dublin in 1640. Burnell was a member of the confederate Assembly. See Dix, 'Plays printed in Ireland before 1701', *Irish Book Lover* (March–April 1929), 36–7.

offered evidence. The frequent stage directions calling for music and dancing would, however, seem redundant in a play not intended for the stage.[37] Torture scenes and supernatural apparitions closely similar to those in Burkhead's script were in fact staged in many Stuart plays, within a flourishing popular-theatre culture in which realism was not the norm. Furthermore, the masque tradition which developed in Britain from the Jacobean and throughout the Caroline period, right up to the eve of the First English Civil War, involved high production values and the development of sophisticated technical apparatus. The contemporary scholarship of Caroline theatre would reject the closet-drama view, and see nothing in *Cola's furie* to preclude its being staged.[38]

*Theatre contexts in Ireland: audience*
Whether or not it was ever performed, *Cola's furie* draws, by the very fact of its existence and generic self-positioning, upon both literary and dramatic conventions. There are several possible contexts in Irish theatre history for its composition and perhaps production. From 1637 until the outbreak of rebellion in October 1641 there had, of course, been a professional theatre company in Dublin. This was the Werburgh St. Theatre, managed by John Ogilby under the auspices of the court of Strafford, then viceroy.[39] Most study of Strafford in Ireland has been exclusively political, but he was a collector of pictures, a lover of plays and an enthusiastic patron, and the culture of his court is now attracting long-overdue investigation.[40] The resident dramatist at Werburgh Street was James Shirley, and apart from his own plays – *The Royal Master, Rosania; or, Love's victory,* and *St Patrick for Ireland* – it is known that works by Jonson, Fletcher, and Middleton were performed there. The bulk of the audience for this theatre, which corresponds in character to the private theatres in London, must have been made up of the Dublin upper and upper-middle classes, largely Catholic and Old English. Many men from these very groups were subsequently members of the confederate General Assembly in Kilkenny between 1642 and 1648. Though Shirley complains bitterly in his prologues of the inadequacy of

---

37  As is remarked by Dale Randall, *Winter Fruit,* p. 92.
38  I thank my colleague James Knowles for illuminating discussion of the performance potential of *Cola's furie* in the light of theatre-history research over the past two decades.
39  See Clark, *Early Irish stage,* pp 26–43; A.H. Stevenson, 'James Shirley and the actors at the first Irish theatre', *Modern Philology,* 40 (1942), 149–55 and 'Shirley's Years in Ireland', *Review of English Studies* 20 (1944), 19–28; J. Turner (ed.), *St Patrick for Ireland* (New York, 1979). There is further discussion of Shirley in Dublin in Patricia Coughlan, '"Cheap and common animals": the English anatomy of Ireland in the seventeenth century', in Thomas Healy and Jonathan Sawday (eds), *Literature and the English Civil War* (Cambridge, 1990), 205–223; Deana Rankin, *Between Spenser and Swift: English writing in seventeenth-century Ireland* (Cambridge, 2005), pp 96–108.
40  See for instance Dougal Shaw, 'Thomas Wentworth and monarchical ritual in early Modern Ireland', *Historical Journal* 49:2 (2006), 331–55.

the support offered by these audiences and of their lack of aesthetic discernment, the fact remains that they had had first-hand exposure over four years or so to regular performances of classic and modern plays in the English tradition. In Aylward's prefatory verses commending *Cola's furie,* Burkhead's work is compared to that of Jonson, Shakespeare, and Beaumont and Fletcher; 'The most admired Sherly and the crew/Of English Dramaticks cry hayle to you', he writes. Breede's verses also invoke the names of major contemporary artists:

> Had Rubens and Vandike liv'd and at strife,
> Who should pourtray best Cola to the life,
> Their curious Art, the way could never find
> To Paint his body as thy Muse his minde.

### Local theatre contexts

There were also local contexts for *Cola's furie* in the form of Kilkenny's special dramatic traditions. Besides the fairly rudimentary folk mummers' plays surviving in the east and south-east of Ireland, this included the open-air miracle play which, since the mid-sixteenth century, been performed in the city's public places on Corpus Christi and Midsummer Day; this was still being done in 1639, only three years before the confederation began to meet. These performances may have originated with the Protestant proselytizing drama of Bishop John Bale in the 1550s.[41] The plays were based on the stories of the Resurrection, the Temptation, and the Nine Worthies, and their characters included not only Christ, Mary, and Michael the Archangel, but Hector, Charlemagne, Satan, and another demon called Belphegor, a comic devil or vice-figure (whom it is tempting to consider a possible antecedent for the characterization of the evil Cola).

There is another known strand to Kilkenny's theatre life, almost exactly contemporary with *Cola's furie.* The Jesuits set up a college there in 1642 as part of the post-Tridentine expansion of their international, prospectively worldwide, mission, and at least one play was produced in 1644. A very elaborate and informative playbill advertising this production survives.[42] It was a religious drama called *Titus; or, The palme of Christian courage,* a play drawn from the history of the Jesuit mission to Japan and strongly Counter-Reformation in flavour, rehearsing the steadfast resistance of the hero to threats of persecution and martyrdom. Between the main scenes of prison, threatened torture, and heroic defiance, however, there are 'Interludes' which seem to be low and comic in

41  Clark, *Early Irish stage,* pp 22–3; Alan Fletcher, *Drama, performance, and polity in pre-Cromwellian Ireland* (Cork, 2000), pp 161–97, discusses this tradition and the concrete evidence of its equipment, props, and staging at length.

42  The playbill is in the Bradshaw collection of Cambridge University Library. It has been discussed by Kavanagh (*Irish theatre,* pp 47–55), and at length by Kerrigan (pp 188–92).

flavour, bearing a loose relation to the plot, and involving low characters – common brutish soldiers and thieves. This sharp alternation between high heroic and demotic textures is characteristic also of Burkhead's play.

Furthermore, it seems that there were dramatic performances of some description mounted in Kilkenny during the period of the confederation, and that the confederation authorities practised considerable ceremony both ecclesiastical and secular. The pomp greeting the papal delegate Cardinal Rinuccini in November 1645 is an example. He was met by a formal procession among which were a group of fifty mounted students from the Jesuit college. These, 'after caracoling round me, conveyed their compliments to me though one of their number, a youth crowned with laurel and in a richer habit than the rest, and who recited some verses to me'.[43] Grandeur in liturgy and vestments and a stress on outward and visible religious performance were, of course, hallmarks of Counter-Reformation Catholicism, then an important influence on Irish practice.[44]

The contemporary account of the confederation in the *Aphorismical discovery* refers specifically to stage plays. In September 1642 when Thomas Preston arrived from the Netherlands, his wife and daughters were feted and

> arrivinge were served with dayly invitations, feasts and banquetts with the varietie as well of pallat-inticinge dishes, as of gratulatorie poems, civill and martiall representations of comedies and stage playes, with mightie content.[45]

As is apparent in the extract's ironic tone, this is a hostile account: its author, writing after the Cromwellian invasion and the ultimate catastrophic outcome, supported Owen Roe O'Neill and the native Irish and was bitterly opposed to what he perceived as the Old English domination of the confederation with its constant treating with Ormond; he was also scornful of Preston's abilities. Here he equates the plays with the 'palate-enticing dishes', and elsewhere attacks the literary pretensions of Richard Bellings, secretary to the confederation's supreme council and author of a continuation of Sidney's *Arcadia*.

## V: AESTHETICS AND POLITICS: 'COLA'S FURIE' AS LITERATURE
### EMBLEMATIC CHARACTERIZATIONS

As I have argued, *Cola's furie* does not answer to a realist reading, which characteristically emphasizes a strongly individuated and coherent subjectivity and

---

43  G. Aiazza (ed.), *Embassy*, 90.

44  See Corish, *Irish Catholic experience*, and John Bossy, 'The Counter-Reformation and the people of Catholic Ireland', in *Historical Studies*, 8 (1971), 155–69.

45  Anon., *Aphorismical discovery of treasonable faction*, John T. Gilbert (ed.), in *A contemporary history of affairs in Ireland from 1641 to 1652*, i, pt 1 (Dublin, 1879), 46.

therefore values characters who give the illusion of possessing psychological depth. Hence, no doubt, much of Kavanagh's scorn for the play. Its characters, even Cola, are defined not primarily by emotional interiority or self-analysis. Rather they *are* their, morally fixed, roles: Cola the inexplicably deranged villain, Abner the good general, divinely approved, Theodorike the god-gifted commander (the meaning of his Greek-derived name). The minor characters are emblems of heroism or brutality, called into being for their necessary moment.[46] The play is a study of violent human actions, sometimes as performed and sometimes as suffered, but always as given their ultimate meaning by the historical – and historic – struggle going on, which is itself represented as a moral conflict between good and evil. This, as I have argued, determines the piece's episodic structure: it is a parade of many brief scenes. The concentration on political passions and imperatives leaves no room for private motive; but to consider this as an impoverishment is to misunderstand Burkhead's whole project.

Only in the case of Cola's characterization may there be a possible exception to this flatness – itself the norm in the drama of the period, as for example in the extensive canon of Beaumont and Fletcher tragicomedies which dominated fashionable theatre in the pre-Civil War decades. Cola is represented as in the grip of a dementia, the 'fury' of the title, which is rationally inexplicable and causes him to multiply senseless cruelties against the Lirendeans. This uncontrollable rage sets him apart from the other Angoleans in the play, with the possible exception of Tygranes, who at the end of the fifth act of *Cola's furie* is just promising wholesale massacre when he is killed by the cannon shot. Significantly, Cola has been shot at the end of Act iv, so Tygranes has in a sense taken over his malevolent role and functions as his double.

Cola is distinguished from the others not just by greater ruthlessness, but also by social inferiority. On his first appearance he speaks a soliloquy after the leaders' exit, which in a sense gives him a psychological motivation, but as much against his own party as the enemy:

> My hearts
> as good as theirs, had I equall power, Ide
> teare the fabricke of this world asunder;
> my fury like *Joves* violent thunder
> should blast the earth farre worse than *Phaeton*
> in his heedles course. What would I not have done,
> what Kingdomes ransackt till I had my will
> of these on whom I ground my hatred still. (i, 307–14)

---

46 Catherine Belsey calls this 'emblematic' rather than 'illusionist' psychology; it was widely used in Renaissance texts, for instance in Ben Jonson's characterizations, and draws on the theory of humours.

In conceiving this figure, Burkhead was surely influenced, as I have suggested earlier, by Senecan figures, but this was overlaid by the malcontent types of Elizabethan and Stuart theatre, who were often imagined by their English creators as Machiavellian – Webster's Bosola and Shakespeare's Iago, for instance. But he was also drawing on actuality. Coote's low origins and taste for brutality are scornfully noted and their alleged connection asserted in the following anecdote from the *Aphorismical discovery*. It describes the chill reception given him in March 1642, after the raising of the rebels' unsuccessful siege of Drogheda, by Ormond, the earl of Antrim, and Antrim's wife who had been duchess of Buckingham:

> That humaine-bloudsucker, Sir Charles Coote ... bragginge too much of that daies service, Ormond and both the other earles silent, but the duttchesse took upon her to answeare him, as both Englishe and better acquainted with his good genius, tould him what he was, a poore mecanicall fellow, raised by blind fortune, as enformer and promoter, against all that is iust and godly, beinge chiefe instrument of the shedinge of many inocent bloude, and of the comencement of the now distempers; that the Irish was more loyall to the crowne of England; very bad language she gave him, to this tune ...      (*Aphorismical discovery*, vol. i, 31)

In the play Cola seems almost to suffer his rage rather than being the agent of it.[47] In the third act of *Cola's furie*, just after the scene where he has Cephalon and Rufus racked, he soliloquizes: 'What Hercules can remove this mountaine / of enraged passions from my heart?' The very embodiment of fury ('Enter Cola, his weapon drawne'), incapable of self-analysis but compelled by an insane force, he plans 'to hang, to racke, to kill, to burne, to spoile / untill I make this land a barren soile' (ii, 62–3). The Lirendeans explicitly call him 'Machavillian', as well as comparing him to 'a demidivell or Cannibal' crying out 'kill, kill'. As a character, he is uninflected, headlong, absolute, resembling a personification of anger in a medieval morality text or an allegory, who cannot get outside the quality he is doomed endlessly to represent. Yet his very energy is imaginatively compelling, a point I shall return to.

*Providence and supernatural manifestations*
Burkhead's resort to notions of the direct intervention in human affairs of fate, or providence, also strongly resembles what happens in English drama of the 1640s. Such interpretations of human struggles were resorted to partly, no doubt, under the pressure of civil strife. For example, the hero Abner (preposterously representing the militarily underwhelming Preston), on his first appearance in

---

47 Kerrigan perceptively observes the half-pun in his name on the Greek borrowing 'choler', which meant 'rage' in the period.

[ 26 ]

the play, is cast into a magic sleep. During this, the 'Queene of fates' dances around him with her nymphs, and the gods enter, promising to aid 'the discontented *Lirendeans*' (iv, 109). On this occasion Abner is dispirited: he has entered reading a letter which gives bad news about his sons; this probably refers to the capture at Rathconnell of his son, known as Don Diego. (Strengthening the sense of his divinely sanctioned status, Burkhead's name for Preston comes from King Saul's 'captain of the host' in the book of Samuel, who is called 'a valiant man' by David, and is among those divinely cast into an enchanted sleep). The biblical Abner, like Burkhead's in the last act of the play, calls (though more eloquently) for an end to fighting:

> Then Abner called to Joab, and said, Shall the sword devour for ever? knowest thou not that it will be bitterness in the latter end? how long shall it be then, ere thou bid the people return from following their brethren?

At his death, David ceremoniously laments him, with great honour and signs of grief (I Samuel 17.55, 26.7–15, II Samuel 2.14–32, 3.28–39). Further, during the concluding battle of the play, the vicious Angolean general Tygranes is made to express a sense that the Lirendean victory is indeed fated:

> All will not doe, some horrible wicked
> destinie befriends them; our men drop downe
> on every side, whereat they seeme to scoffe,
> and floute ...                                    (v, 328–31)

Coherent and effective human will is thus resigned to supernatural destiny and, as we see strikingly in the fourth act of *Cola's furie*, both Abner and Cola are acted upon by greater forces which intervene materially by manifesting themselves on the stage – the gods Mars, Bellona, Pallas and Mercury, and a figure of Revenge, 'followed', retributively, by 'three Spirits in sheets'. This supernatural management of affairs by means of purely emblematic, metaphysical figures was much used in Elizabethan plays, and remained prominent in the politically oppositional repertoire of the London popular theatres right up to the Civil War.[48] It is interesting to note the common reliance, both by the Catholic Burk-

---

48  See Martin Butler, *Theatre and crisis*, pp 81, 189: '"the red bull phrase", said John Cleveland mockingly, "was enter three devils *solus*"' (the Red Bull being looked down upon by some as one of the public theatres). This recalls Burkhead's haunting of Cola by the three spirits in sheets. See also Michael Hattaway, *Elizabethan popular theatre* (London, 1987), pp 32–3, 114–15. In *A looking glass for London and England* (1590) 'A hand from out a cloud threatens with a burning sword' (32); similarly, Burkhead's character Revenge says to Cola: 'This bloodie sword and flaming torch are them / true Emblems of thy furious stratageme ...'

head and by Protestant patriotic dramatists of the Jacobean and Caroline periods, on the notion of providence and the device of unearthly intervention: an imaginative enlistment of transcendent backing which seeks to circumvent the reality of political powerlessness, though on opposite sides. The supernatural was regularly summoned in plays both sophisticated and popular. The retributive haunting of Cola, in our example, is a motif which is common to 'high' Elizabethan tragedies such as *Julius Caesar* – Burkhead's scene is strongly reminiscent of Caesar's phantom visitation of Brutus in his tent before Philippi – and to the political pamphlet plays of the Civil War period, which sometimes wishfully represent Cromwell, Fairfax or other Parliamentary leaders as terrified by the visits of indignant ghosts.[49]

In the case of Cola, Burkhead may have been drawing also on folk accounts of Coote's death. The narrative of this event in the *Aphorismical discovery* links it with a specific impiety in a way that suggests such accounts were current:

> his son Ricc Coote, (qualis arbor, talis fructus) hitted upon a great ancient portraiture, or image of Our Blessed Ladie engraven in wood, kept with great veneration in the same house since the supression of holy churche in Henry the 8 his time, which younge Coote caused to be cutt and cloven in sunder, to make fire therof for his father against his cominge in. Butt God Allmight, the righteous judge, did not prolonge the punishment of this impietie, for as soon as Sir Charles thought to enjoy the benefitt of that transformed-divine fire, worde came to him that the Irish alreadie intred the towne ... Sir Charles was shott or otherwise wounded, and makinge as much examination in this behalf as reasonablie I might, could never learne how or by whom was he soe wounded, how ever, it beinge mortall, was conveyed to his lodginge deade. (vol. i, 32)

The marginal gloss says, as if to clinch the point: 'Not known how killed unlesse by a miracle.'

Nevertheless, perhaps because of the chronicle-like character of Burkhead's material, the empirical events stubbornly retain their accidental quality even against his desire to subsume them into the supernatural plan of justice and deserved retribution. One aspect of this may be that the kind of war being fought in the 1640s obtrudes its modernity on the traditional procedures of gallantry and single combat which prevail in the quasi-heroic theatre representation of war. It is important that Cola's death at the climax of Act iv and Tygranes' at the end of Act v are both produced from a distance, by a pistol and a cannon shot respectively, and are thus shorn of the dignity and personal directness of

49  The royalist play *Crafty Cromwell* is one which does this; see Janet Clare's 'Introduction' to her *Drama of the English Republic*.

sword-fighting. As a result, Burkhead's probable intention – to show the deserved fate of such abhorrent figures – may seem to the modern eye to be overridden by a sense of randomness and the haphazard.

The attempt to recuperate this randomness by presenting it as the intervention of providence is lent a somewhat desperate quality by our inescapable hindsight about the eventual disastrous outcome for the confederates and their supporters. For all its emotional poignancy, therefore, it is hard for us now to experience Burkhead's deployment of this device of supernatural sanctions to validate his moral and political judgements as anything more than the product of desperation. The vindicating visitations of the gods and of Revenge and the final angel of peace who appears 'to perclose the Scaene' in the final act of *Cola's furie* cannot cancel the reader's more forceful impression of disorder and brutality prevailing, and of the ultimate absence of a redressing Providence. Yet what Burkhead has attempted is to substitute in *fantasy* (that is, the action of his play) Cola's rage and Abner's fatedness for the political contentions prevailing in *actuality* (the action of history), and thus to bring about a *metaphysical* resolution of the *material* conflict of military powers.

*The 'low' characters*

The figures of the common soldiers are realized with a vividness which counterweighs the insubstantiality of the metaphysical invocations in the play. The characters represented are mostly homogeneous in social status and language – gentlemen, ladies and aristocrats – with the possible exception among the commanders, as we have seen, of Cola himself. But Cola uses the same register of language – high and heavily laced with classical allusion – and the same (metrically loose) verse as the other generals and 'Governors'. Outside this group Burkhead does, however, represent two others: one, very briefly suggested, consists of the citizens, probably of Dublin and evidently Protestant and prosperous, who, at the beginning of the play, are used to ventilate the plot by expressing their alarm about the rising. The other, more fully represented, is that of the Angolean common soldiers and the peasants and maidservant who are, or nearly are, their victims. Burkhead's imaginative interest in this group is evident from the fairly extended scene they are given in the third act of *Cola's furie*, and their reintroduction in Act v at the defeat of the Angoleans. Their appearances in Act iii are interspersed between the racking of Rufus and Cephalon, a ranting speech by Cola, and the torture of Barbazella, and in one sense they form part of an extended narrative of the inhumanities of the Angoleans as a whole. Thus the soldiers are shown committing indiscriminate robbery, harassing terrified countrymen and attempting to rape Ellenora. But the atmosphere and language of the scene are that of robust low comedy, recalling the 'Interludes' in the Kilkenny Jesuit play *Titus,* and also the scene in Shirley's *St Patrick for Ireland* in which the noblewoman Emeria, like Burkhead's Ellenora, is almost assaulted by a pair of wisecracking soldiers.[50] The effect of the soldiers' presence is predominantly one of robust low comic relief, even when they are threatening the two 'country-men' whom they have caught stealing bags of salt in the sacked town. Presumably Burkhead's sympathies lie with these two hapless characters, but the effect is scarcely one of pathos. The reason for this may be that the two do not grasp the situation, their knowledge of English being inadequate. As they are haled off to be hanged, they incoherently ask: 'Where master? ... I trow no, for what *Agra?'* (iii, 175, 177) – but Burkhead, true to what seems his English rather than Gaelic background, shows no particular feeling for the specifically linguistic element of their plight. *(A ghrá* means 'my love', 'dear', in Irish). He shows the soldiers as decidedly not part of the heroic struggle going on between the more noble-minded of their leaders. They sing derisive songs about the Lord Justice ('Pitho is doting; we don't care who knows it ...') and complain trenchantly about the material discomforts of their lives:

> ... need never so payd in our dayes
> with mouldie scraps of cheese and butter with
> as many collours as the rainbow in't. (iii, 372–4)

And in the last act, when they are defeated, their one desire is to go home: 'an yee be wise not a word of fighting more', and significantly, Burkhead gives them the motive of land acquisition for their presence in Ireland in the first place:

> An I could to my granam once againe,
> I'de ne're come looke for land in Stelern [= Leinster] more.     (v, 94–5)

They are rough and indiscriminate; when a 'gentleman' enters they first beg from, then threaten, and finally 'rifle him', after the following comic exchange, itself deploying an irony bitterly familiar in internecine conflicts at all periods:

> GENTLEMAN I am a Protestant.
> SOULDIERS Be what you will, all's one to us sweet Sir. (iii, 457–8)

There is a liveliness about Burkhead's imagining of these soldiers – and of the only adversary who can stand up to them in repartee and strong will, the maid-servant who preserves her mistress' goods and her own person safe from their attentions (iii, 422–45) – which is otherwise evident only in the characterization of Cola, the embodiment of energy and motion in the play.

---

50 The first Interlude in *Titus*: 'A Country Clowne, hearing that a proclamation was to issue against the Christians, is mightily merry, and attempts to rob a passenger' (quoted in Kavanagh, *Irish theatre*, p. 51; see discussion, Section II above). The scene in *St Patrick for Ireland* is v. i.

*The female characters*

There are six female characters, all on the Lirendean side and all relatively minor, three of whom make only one, quasi-communal, appearance in the first act of *Cola's furie*. The other three, Ellenora, Barbazella and a maidservant, are subjected respectively to threatened rape, torture, and, in a quasi-comic vein, attempted robbery, robustly resisted. No obvious historical equivalents for any of these characters suggest themselves, which is not very surprising: the women, like the common folk of either sex and the soldiers, fill supporting roles in the society of the play, an arrangement not unique to Burkhead. In realist texts the female characters may still function as a repository, site and occasion of the heroes' private feeling, but are also conceived as themselves possessing interior selves (to greater or lesser degrees, of course, even in some much later 'classic realist' texts such as nineteenth-century novels). Here, as I have suggested, they are, to an even greater extent than the male figures, living instances of appropriate abstract qualities who perform prescribed supporting roles. The decorative Florilla, Dulis and Pulchrina duly provide an interlude of encouragement for the 'Nation's gloomy lords' by eliciting gallantries and singing and dancing (i, 384–458). Ellenora almost becomes the sexual prey of the Angolean soldiers in the captured town and thus is the due occasion for the politically required manifestation of their unindividuated moral barbarity (iii, 226–62). At iii, 497–579, Barbazella is strung up and tortured, graphically, by Tygranes – ostensibly for military intelligence, but with the dramatic purpose of providing one more icon of Lirendean steadfastness and vulnerability (however voyeuristic the reader may simultaneously find the spectacle).[51]

*Cola and the villain-hero paradox*

Cola is a very strange compound of empirical fact — we have noted in many instances the play's employment of actual historical incident — and literary type, in the form of a villain-hero. His restlessness and vigour, like those of Milton's Satan and of Marlowe's despot heroes, makes him perversely attractive to the imagination.[52] Burkhead, however unconsciously or inconsistently in political terms, responds to this attraction by finding for Cola by far the most compelling language in the play. Cola's seems the one credibly active will at work in the fiction, however malevolent. He is the only human figure who is felt – though almost in a Sadeian sense – to dominate his environment, the subject with an over-reaching will who goes to work upon others and produces victims. These

51  She is tortured by Tygranes to make her reveal information about the 'plot' of one 'Cornet Brinfort'.

52  The characterization of Cromwell in Marvell's 'Horatian Ode', written four years later, is balanced with more complexity between good and evil, but offers a parallel in being part fated and part self-willed.

– whether they are the old men who are racked, the hanged or massacred peasants or the tortured Barbazella – play the structurally feminine role of Lirendean submission, invoked in the subtitle of the play, to the masculine force of Angola, which Cola most effectively personifies.

Only supernatural intervention could definitively put an end to Lirenda's captivity and griefs; or as Theodorike's dignified lament for his countrymen summarily killed puts it:

> *Lirenda*, poore *Lirenda* now farewell,
> farewell thy former pompe, all's turn'd to griefe
> attired in crimson robes of bloodie death
> that none but heavens compassive motions can
> subdue ... (ii, 385–9)

Beside this overpowering sense of desperation and ubiquitous destruction, the positive ending of the play, with a Lirendean victory and the year and a day's cessation, is rather a shaky and provisional triumph. True to the facts of history, Abner has to insist upon the acceptance of the truce against the resistance of some of his colleagues, who call it 'this needles fond cessation' (v, 394); as we have seen, some in the confederate grouping (including the 'clerical party') bitterly resisted the pressure from Ormond to agree to this and still more to the later 1646 peace, feeling that they should capitalize on their existing strength rather than give a breathing-space to the enemy to regroup. The raggedness of this ending denies 'the telos of harmonic integration' that Brecht wanted in epic theatre, as does the unresolved opposition – present, as I have argued, throughout the play – between, on the one hand, the sense of hopelessness before the irrational force centred in Cola's active hatred, and on the other the desire to insist upon the ultimate victory of those possessing courage and a righteous cause.[53] We cannot know how far Burkhead was authorially in control of this effect. But this does not take away from the poignancy of the contradictions his play can continue to rehearse for readers: however unevenly, the text of *Cola's furie* represents with unparalleled vividness the painful interaction of the literary imagination with the facts of Irish history in the 1640s.

University College Cork
May 2008

---

53 The phrase quoted is from Jonathan Dollimore, *Radical tragedy*, p. 63. Dollimore's later remark, paraphrasing Benjamin on Brecht, also illuminates *Cola's furie*: 'Contradiction is incorporated in the very structure of the epic play rather than simply being ignored or, alternatively, acknowledged but ultimately transcended ... Different genres are juxtaposed, sometimes jarringly so' (64).

# A note on the text

My editorial practice has been guided by an intention to create an edition that is as faithful as possible to the printed text of 1645 (of which there appears to be only one extant copy – in the British Library) whilst still being intelligible to the modern reader. Inconsistencies in spelling within the commendatory verses and the main text of the play have been retained with the following concessions: the words 'then' and 'than' and 'to' and 'too' are amended to their modern forms; the early modern characters 'i' and 'v' (which occur rarely) have been modernized to 'j' and 'u'; the spelling of characters' names in speech prefixes, in the dramatis personae, in stage directions and in the main text of the play has been regularized. I have glossed words where the early modern spelling causes ambiguity that is not clarified by context, as well as archaic words and proverbs.

The most substantial change is in punctuation. In the original printed text pauses and stops are denoted by commas, colons and semi-colons in a manner that may confuse modern readers. In the instances where I have altered the punctuation to clarify the syntax I have, I hope, been sensitive to the rhythm of Burkhead's lines. Question marks and exclamation marks have been added in a few instances where deemed appropriate. Inconsistencies in the italicisation of proper names (people, countries etc.) have been silently corrected.

Burkhead's prosody is uncertain and although in most instances the lines that make up the long speeches and soliloquies are written in pentameters, the short lines do not scan with any consistency. I have therefore avoided re-lineation and retained the original presentation of the text at a left-hand margin.

The stage directions have been reproduced in their entirety, and have been re-punctuated where necessary. Some stage directions, such as those that denote 'asides', have been moved from the right-hand margin and placed in square brackets within the main text.

Angelina Lynch
Dublin, May 2008

COLA'S FURIE

# [DRAMATIS PERSONAE]
## THE NAMES OF THE CHIEFE ACTORS[1]

| | |
|---|---|
| *Pitho and Berosus* | Angolean Governors of Lirenda |
| *Osirus* | Lieutenant Generall of the Angolean Forces |
| *Cola* | Serjeant-Major Generall [the Angolean army] |
| *Tygranes* | A Noble Man |
| *Albinus, Celar and Tibernus* | Angolean Commanders |
| *Belfrida* | A Spie to the Angoleans |
| *Athenio, Mineus, Aretas and Dora* | Noble Men of Lirenda |
| *Theodorike and Lentimos* | Lirendean Commanders |
| *Cephalon and Rufus* | Lirendean Gentlemen |
| *Abner* | Generall of Stelern |
| *Caspilona* | Generall of the [Lirendean] Horse |
| *Lysana* | Generall of the Angolean Horse |
| *Florilla, Dulis and Pulchrina* | Ladies of Lirenda |
| *Ellenora and Barbazella* | Two Gentlewomen |

[Also]

Mars, Pallas, Mercury, Queen of Fates, Bellona and Nymphes
Angolean Soldiers

---

1   Burkhead omitted the character Vavasiro (who appears briefly in Act V, 228) from the *dramatis personae*. For the identification of the characters with historical figures see the Appendix. Lirenda/Lirendean = Ireland/Irish; Angolean = English; Stelern = Leinster.

# TO THE RIGHT HONOURABLE
## EDWARD SOMMERSET
## LORD HERBERT[1]

*Baron Beaufort of Gresmond, Earle of Glamorgan, Son and Heire*
*apparent to the most Honorable* HENRY *Marques of Worcester*

RIGHT HONORABLE,

'Tis a principle of Nature, that Creatures of weake condition, aiming at security, doe direct their course for shelter to the wings of the more potent; so Principalities and states of inferior note doe manifest their sollicitude to gaine the patronage of some Royall Majestie. This little worke, by reason of its meanes, dares not adventure to be exposed to the publique censure unlesse it be protected under the Scepter of Honorable Authority, and whether shall it betake it selfe if not to your Honour, whom God hath established on Earth as a particular image of his glory; assuredly the rayes of honor originally issuing from your countenance, the generall esteeme of your unparaleled worth and your matchlessse zeale and Christian fortitude in your weighty undertakings are no lesse arguments of your incomparable merit than incentives to the learned to adorne their Chronicles with the lustre of your deserts.[2] The subject of this small worke being drawn from the historicall records of Forren countryes, and fitly applyable to the distempers of this Kingdome, may the rather be admitted to the favour of your noble patronage, forasmuch as your Honour, out of the generosity of your nature, have been pleased with a glance of reall compassion to view and survey the modell of its sad afflictions, having with unspeakable toyle, charges and dangers adventured hither (not unlike NOAH'S Dove, with an Olive branche of Peace) to appease the raging fury of our intestine harmes. This enriching the Diademe of your renown with a particular Jewell of rare merit, are not these issues and ofsprings of a boyling & bleeding heart, boyling with impregnable love and loyaltie unto his Majestie, and bleeding for the continuall distempers of his Kingdomes. Pardon then, Right Honorable, the authors presumption, who making humble remonstrance of his reall observance & duest respects, builds not upon the worth of this subject, but wholly relies on the favour of your noble acceptance, assuring himselfe the characters of your name engraven upon its

---

1  Edward Somerset was the Catholic earl of Glamorgan. In 1645 he was sent to Ireland as an envoy of Charles I in order to ensure the quick dispatch of Irish troops to England to aid the royalist army.

2  deserts = merits.

frontispice will not only impart a particular lustre unto it, but will (moreover) yeeld it acceptable to all readers. Why then, as the glittering beames of your unspotted loyaltie (true effects of a generous heart) have given a full reflection on the darke brow of this distracted age, so posteritie hereafter may blesse, praise and admire your zealous noble undertakings, whose felicitie can never equalize the hearty wishes of

Your Honors most humble and most obsequious servant,

HENRY BURKHEAD

*To my loving and respected friend* Mr. Henry Burkhead *Merchant,*
*upon his Tragedie of* COLA'S FURY.


I Once did studie Navigation
Thinking to draw my speculation,
Unto the Practique, when (alas) I found
Safer (than set to Sea) to stay on ground.
  But thou (my friend) upon a faire pretence,
Reserved Art and prosperous Confidence,
Hast lanced[1] forth into a raging tide,
By thee not knowne (till now) nor ever tried.
  Yet got into the mayne, through Cruell Rocks
Trough Read-Sea-Sands, and shelves and boysterous shocks[2]    10
Of murdering billowes, Cumbred with sad feares[3]
Of frighted and self-moaning Passengers,
Do'st steere thy Course. Thy Card and Compasse show[4]
Thou do'st a plaine, smooth and direct line know.
  Thou hast fresh gales and Sea-roome; for who shall[5]
Behold thy dolefull Pinnace rise and fall[6]
Mid'st such deepe dangers (as herein appeares),
Weighing the misery, shall with sighes and teares,
Supplie the *Ocean* with most glad desire,
Sit in thy steerage-roome, will there admire,    20
  Thy new-found skill, and with a dextrous ease
  Learne to sayle with thee, by like Windes and Seas.


    *Thy assured wellwisher,*
    William Smyth[7]


---

1   lanced = launched.
2   The Israelites were forced to cross the Red Sea – properly translated as the 'Sea of Reeds' – to escape from slavery in Egypt. See Exodus 14. 18. Trough = through.
3   billowes [billows] = waves.
4   Card = map / chart.
5   Sea-roome [room] = space at sea free from obstruction.
6   Pinnace= small sailing vessel.
7   Smyth [Smith] may have been the well-known figure who came to Ireland from the west of England in 1630, and who was the associate of the catholic Walter Butler, earl of Ormond. See Introduction.

*To his deere friend* Mr. Henry Burkhead, *upon his*
*Tragedy of Cola's fury.*

Some have writ playes (my *Burkhead*) that have gain'd
A large applause unto themselves, not strayn'd
Nor forc'd, nor hir'd but rightly; it is true
They have deserved more, and more is due
Than can be payd them: some have well exprest
A Politician, others one distrest,
Some lusts and treasons, others Tyranny,
And others some the state and Majestie[1]
Of Lords and Princes; others have well limb'd
Th'extortious Souldier, others neatly trimm'd                    10
The Curious Courtier. But Sir, you portray'd
Each various humour, variously array'd,
And suted so each passion to the life,
*Protheus* we thought had been with you at strife,[2]
who could produce most shapes that we must say,
*Protheus* hath labour'd with you 'bout this play.
What? Though of *Terence, Seneca,* we heare,[3]
And other moderne Scenicks in our spherare,[4]
You I preferred. *Johnson* for all his wit[5]
Could never paint our times as you have hit                     20
The manners of our age. The fame declines
Of ne're enough prays'd *Shakespeare* if thy lines
Come to be publisht; *Beaumont* and *Fletcher's* skill[6]
Submitts to yours, and your more learned quill.
The most admired *Sherly* and the crew[7]
Of *English* Dramaticks cry hayle to you,
*Phebus* choice darling. Sir, I not admire[8][9]
The Muses nurst you, and he was your Sire.

*Paul Aylward*[10]

1  i.e. some others.          2  In Greek mythology Proteus was a shape-changing sea god.
3  Terence (*c.*190–159 BC) and Seneca (*c.*4 BC–AD 65) were Roman dramatists.
4  Scenicks = dramatists; spherare = sphere.
5  Ben Jonson (1572–1637): the poet and dramatist.
6  Francis Beaumont (1584–1616) and John Fletcher (1579–1625) collaborated on several plays.
7  James Shirley (1596–1666) was a leading dramatist who was based at the Werburgh Street Theatre in Dublin from 1636–40.
8  Phoebus (also known as Apollo) was the Greek god of the sun.          9  not = now [?].
10 Aylward was most likely a member of the prominent Clonmel and Waterford family of
   Catholic merchants who were major clients of the Butlers. See Introduction.

To his deere friend the Author on his Tragedie
of *Cola's* fury, or *Lirenda's* misery.

*When first I read your Tragedy and meete*
*Truth, wit, and judgement trip with equall feet,*
*Without th'expence of paines, that all may know*
*They unconstrayned from your pen doe flow.*
*I could not choose but wonder that your braine*
*Without great Arts could hit so high a straine,*
*Such as the power of each line alone*
*Is able to transforme a man to stone.*
*Nor is it strange, when that therein wee see*                    10
*Such bloodie massachers and crueltie,*
*As doth transcend what cruell* Nero *and*[1]
*Great* Dyonisus *acted in each land;*[2]
*Had* Rubens *and* Vandike *liv'd and at strife*[3]
*Who should pourtray best* Cola *to the life,*
*Their curious Art the way could never find*
*To Paint his body as thy Muse his minde.*
*Thou hast so lively him exprest that I*
*Reading was rapt into an extasie,*
*But straight againe perplext with so great feare*
*As if that cruell* Cola *present were.*                         20
*Deere friend, since then this peece so well limn'd*[4]
*As most would thinke 'twas by* Ben Johnson *trimm'd,*
*That* Shakespeare, Fletcher *and all did combine*
*To make* Lirenda *through the Clouds to shine.*
*Enfranchise her, and let her come th'view*
*Of publique Censure, where the best (be sure)*
*Will give her welcomes such as shall endure,*
*Els as a Miser you'le be understood*
*That hoords up gold, and does the poore no good;*
*Feare not the Zoyly nor the Criticke faces*[5]                  30

1   Nero (AD 37–68) the Roman emperor who was infamous for his cruelty.
2   The Greek god Dionysus (known by the Romans as Bacchus) was associated with madness
    and violent cults. He also became linked with the theatre.
3   The renowned Flemish painters Peter Paul Rubens (1577–1640) and Anthony Van Dycke
    (1599–1641).
4   limn'd = portrayed.
5   Zoyly = most likely a plural form of Zoilus meaning a censorious or envious critic. The
    eponymous term derives from the Greek grammarian famous for his criticism of Homer.

*That barke and snarle at th'Muses and the Graces,*[6]
*Their anticque mouthes and squinted eyes shall be*
*Stopt and obscur'd when they* Lirenda *see*
*Breake through the mists of Envy and dispence*
*Light, vigour, Motion and intelligence*
*To all that Candid art, whose votes shall Crowne*
*The* Worke *and* Author *with a smile not frowne,*
*And to augment the Trophies of thy prayse*
*Impale thy browes with wreathes of* Delphique *bayes.*[7]

Daniel Breede

<hr>

6  In classical mythology the nine Muses and the three Graces were goddesses who presided over
   the realms of the arts and of beauty respectively.
7  In classical mythology the oracle at Delphi inhaled burning bay (or laurel) leaves to bring on
   her visionary trances. Wreathes made from laurel leaves were often given as a reward to a conqueror or a poet. See Horace, *Odes and Epodes*, 3. 30.

# THE PROLOGUE

Some Prologues wish their Audience joyfull mirth,
Some with Appelles strive to Painte the birth[1]
Of their inventions; others not onely true,
But pleasing to the kinde spectators view;
Such would our Author too had not his Muse
A mournfull subject whom this age abuse.
Nor can his Novice genius dive unto
The depth of what hee faine would tender you:
Lirenda's Misery, who can forbeare,
The Scene once past, from a relenting teare,          10
When blustring stormes of murder, fire and sword
Are the chiefe Emblems hee can best afford
Your true compassive fancie; looke not then for
A Poets loftie dazeling Meteor,
That to the vulgar eye might seeme more strange
Than fertile Luna in hir often change.
Kinde Natives of this poore afflicted Ile,
To your oppressions we addresse the style
Of this our tragicke pen, who in effect,
Are the supporters of that Architect,                 20
Devised by him that never writ before,
Yet honors you, your miseries adore.
Your faithful service, resolution and
The most accomplisht vertues of this land,
Sometime styl'd Insula Sanctorum,[2]
Now the true touchstone or decorum
Of Heroicall mindes, whom envyes dire intent
Endeavour'd to subvert with discontent.
This, Noble, Worthy Auditors, the scope
Of what wee are resolv'd to shew, in hope             30
Your frequent goodnesse with attentive care,
Our more imperfect lines will mildly beare,
For which the Muses humbly we desire,
Some heavenly rapture may your thoughts inspire.

---

1  Apelles was a famous painter of ancient Greece.
2  Insula Sanctorum = Island of the Saints: a name given to Ireland on account of its famous
   monasteries.

# COLA'S FURIE
## OR
## LIRENDA'S
## MISERIE


## ACT I


*Enter a Constable and two Soldiers with halberts.*°

1 SOLDIER  Must not a Creature passe?
CONSTABLE  No; that's the scoape
    of our Commission. Stand; who comes there?     *Enter a Citizen.*
CITIZEN  A friend.
CONSTABLE  The Word                                         5
CITIZEN  Marry Sirs, God blesse us all.
CONSTABLE  Well spoken, yet you must not passe.
CITIZEN  Not passe?
    Then if you be good fellows, let us chat
    a while; prethee, what means this sudden tumult?     10
CONSTABLE  The matter seemes so strange to me as yet
    we can returne no other answere but
    the state, on paine of death, commands all men
    (thus ready arm'd) to stand upon their guard.
1 SOLDIER  You may be sure there's some rancke plot in hand,     15
    or would the State at these unusuall houres
    sit in a private Councell else?
CITIZEN  'Twish a fable;°
    'tis but some dronken quarrel thus disturbes
    our rest, or the field appointed by some°     20
    hot furious gallant whereto the State
    will not give way.
CONSTABLE  Be it the same, wee'll not
    remove from hence, nor you in dutie ought
    to sleight the matter thus, as if your worships     25
    wisedome were so ripe to apprehend the cause.
CITIZEN  You cannot give more likelier reasons for't.

---

[Stage Direction] halbert = a military weapon; a combination of a spear and a battleaxe.
[18] 'Twish = I wish it were [?]
[20] field = battlefield.

CONSTABLE  Y'are mistaken friend; the common report's
    abroad farre different from your conceit;
    rais'd to the highest point of a distracted              30
    mutiny wee wote not what to thinke or speake,°
    such is the horrid treacherie intended.
CITIZEN  Good Lord forbid; 'gainst whom?
CONSTABLE  This City Castle;°
    and by a few of Romish Recusants°               35
    thinke to subvert the true reformed Gospell.
CITIZEN  How? Our owne fast friends? That were a jest indeed
    past my beliefe.
CONSTABLE  Be not incredulous.
CITIZEN  How can I choose               40
    but frame my thoughts like a confused Chaos.
    To thinke these men who by exterior signes
    and loving conversations threw their hearts
    into our armes; nay more I might expresse
    but that I see all proves a feigned friendship,       45
    and our joynt love's turn'd to a mortall hate.
CONSTABLE  'Tis much, much feared wee'll find it so e're long,
    written in Characters of blood.
I SOLDIER  Silence;
    the Lords themselves doe come to give their best      50
    advice.

*Enter Pitho, Berosus, Mayor* [and] *Recorder.*°

PITHO  Wee call'd you hether to make knowne
    the danger that now, even now, is reveal'd;
    wherefore so true we conceive you be, that
    with all speed you goe unto each port and see      55
    them strongly guarded, with strict command that
    none on paine of death shall issue forth until
    a true & perfect search be made throughout
    this Citie; for as we credibly are inform'd,
    *Guyrua* with all his rude conspirators°      60

[31] i.e. we know not what to …
[34] City Castle = Dublin Castle, the administrative centre of government in Ireland.
[35] Recusants = Those people (most commonly Catholics) who refused to attend the services of the Churches of England or Ireland.
[Stage Direction] Recorder = magistrate.
[60] Guyrua may refer to Maguire, the native Irish Ulster chieftain and prominent leader of the 1641 Rising in Ulster. See Appendix.

are at this instant in a doubtfull feare
to be discovered: the guilt of such a heynous
fact doubtlesse betrayes them. Worthy friends, then
slake not your endeavours; the hast which this°
great businesse now requires admitts no leisure                    65
to stirre your willingnesse with th' effectual
speech of our just cause, that toucheth not your
persons only, but aymes at the Crowne of        *High Treason.*
our dread Soveraigne, and to imbase this°
Kingdomes glory beneath the hollow concave                         70
of their *Papish faction*. This we thought fit
to adde unto your now intended care,
not doubting yours, nor these your brethrens love
to him this waightie matter most concernes.
RECORDER  Sir, we really intend (far from vaine glory              75
be it spoken) to uphold this Cities
ancient fame, that hitherto hath noblie
borne the tytle of a pure unspotted towne.
When treason came as nie to cut you off,°      *1534?*
our fidelity did then expulse your foes,
and with the trophies of their bloodie spoyle                      80
return'd victorious: this we did, and are
as willing yet to manifest the same
so farre as heart and life can shew the dutie
of allegiance.                                                     85
BEROSUS  Them Noble acts renders°
you famous to posterity, nor did
th' Angolean princes prove ungratfull
for that service, as your faire City charter°
can approve.                                                       90
RECORDER  It is acknowledg'd their royall
bounty, wherefore we that doe live will strive
to give as great a lustre to th' Angolean
nation as our renowned ancestors

[64] slake = mitigate / abate; hast = haste.
[69] imbace = embase / bring down.
[79–82] This may refer to the uprising of 'Silken Thomas', i.e. Thomas Fitzgerald, the son of the
earl of Kildare, who besieged Dublin Castle with 15,000 men in 1534. The city authorities with-
stood the insurgents' attack and were rewarded with a grant awarding them the possessions of the
dissolved All Hallows monastery.
[86] On the grammatical significance of the usage 'them', see Introduction.
[89–90] See note to lines 79–82 above.

have done: in this we rest. O Lord decree                    95
our willing powers may curb this treacherie.

*Exeunt omnes preter Pitho [and] Berosus.*

PITHO  Now kinde brother, your grave experience
    must direct what is most needful to be done.
BEROSUS  The chiefest care whereto our watchfull eye
    should bar from future mischiefe: this strong fort°    100
    by heavens protection is secured, therein disabling
    our insulting foes hence forward to proceed.
PITHO  Then are our feares extinct?
BEROSUS  Not so, deere Sir.
    The tempest threatens our ruin still, for              105
    'tis a maxime warlike leaders use, not
    to despise the weaknesse of their foes which
    else might give advantage to their designe,°
    as many woefull presidents there are°
    within the limitts of my youthfull dayes               110
    (too tedious now to nominate) for sixtie
    odde yeares past, since first I practis'd arms in
    the Hiberean warres, when Tyrona, ledd on by°
    some vaine prophesie or other, did strive
    by dint of sword to assure himself the Northern        115
    Crowne with much expence of blood at length°
    t'th Angolean forces cool'd his pride, and made his°
    haughtie courage stoope unto a base ignoble
    flight; yet now me thinks the terrour of this°
    sudden hell-bred newes strikes neere my heart than°    120
    all the legions of his furious traine could
    at that instant when Black-water-Fort prov'd°
    fatall to the most and best of ours.

[100] bar = prevent; strong fort = Dublin Castle.
[107–8] i.e. to overestimate the weakness of your enemy is to give them an advantage …
[109] presidents = precedents.
[113] Tyrona refers to the earl of Tyrone, Hugh O'Neill (*c*.1550–1616), the main antagonist in the Nine Years War (1593–1603), which was waged (unsuccessfully) against the English.
[115–6] Northerne Crowne = rule in Ulster.
[117] t'th = until the.
[119] After the failure of the Nine Years War Tyrone fled Ireland for the continent, eventually settling in Rome on a papal pension.
[120] neere = neerer.
[122] Blackwater Fort in county Armagh was home to an English garrison before being destroyed

PITHO  We then like prudent Statesmen must observe
    some fit occasion may endeere the Palans°             125
    to side with us, until our powers encrease
    with new supplyes from the grand Parliament.
BEROSUS  Your advice is good,
    but were the valiant stout *Osiris* here,
    we then could best proceed; yet fearing least          130
    the pilfring Mountaniers doe fire the suburbs,°
    'twere not amisse if we employed that warlike
    leader brave *Carola Cola*, with whom five
    hundred of our best and ablest men, to front
    the foe at home. Now friend, from whence thy newes?    135

*Enter a Post with letters.*

POST  From *Adrohna.*°    Drogheda
PITHO  How fares the Governor?
POST  In health, an please your Lordship.    [*Pitho & Berosus*] peruse the letters.
BEROSUS  Is the noble Lord *Tygranes* in safetie?
POST  The same my Lord.    140
BEROSUS  It must not be difer'd a minute longer.°
    Goe hast thee to the governor againe,
    and tell him six hundred men completely
    arm'd shall forthwith march to strengthen him,
    and further bid him be of comfort; he    145
    shall not want what's needful.°
POST  I will not faile
    to returne your Lordships answer.
BEROSUS  Brother,
    we must withdraw to hasten what is promist,    150
    we should incurre a lasting scandal else.    *Exeunt.*

---

in 1595 by Hugh O'Neill (see note to line 113) in the course of the Nine Years War.
[125] endeere = induce; Palans = residents of the Pale.
[131] Mountaniers = this may refer to the residents of County Wicklow, known for its mountainous terrain.
[136] Androhna may refer to the town of Drogheda which came under siege from the insurgents following the outbreak of the rising in October 1641. Lord Moore of Melifont (Tygranes) was responsible for the defense of Drogheda until Sir Henry Tichbourne (Tibernus), who had been appointed governor of the city, arrived on 4 November. See Appendix.
[141] difer'd = deferred.
[146] i.e. he shall receive what is needed …

*A march is beaten. Enter Athenio, Mineus, Aretas, Dora, Theodorike and Lentimos.*

*[handwritten: Antrim?]*

ATHENIO  Now that our army is advanch'd thus farre°
    within the confines of our trembling foes,
    whilst yet their scattered troupes lye all dismaid,°
    wee'l pitch a field in view of yon proud towne,°       155
    and stoutly summon them within to yield
    or traine them forth, moved with a bould defiance,°
    wherein wee may expresse an ardent zeale
    to right our natives slavery, and stop
    the current of their puritan designe       160
    intended for our totall ruine.

*[handwritten: Cf. with Confederates accusation that the Puritan Parliament was treasonous.]*

MINEUS  Brave man at armes, thy invincible spirit
    adds more furie to the justnesse of our cause
    than when I recollect a memory
    of *Guyrua's* sad misfortune through some prodigious       165
    starre ominus to poore *Lirenda* still;
    yet if undanted resolution may°
    advance the drooping state of this our native
    clime, let him not prosper will not prosecute
    that base, perfidious, Puritanicall       170
    faction: enemies to God, our mild
    and gracious Soveraigne.

*[handwritten: Counter-discourse]*

ARETAS  I will not boast what
    my intentions are, nor derive an active
    power from my owne selfe conceit. No, Noble       175
    friends and fellow peeres in armes, my ambition's
    fixt on them powers above from whence I
    have a heart both true and loyall, consecrated
    to the service of this pious warre, in
    proofe whereof (vouchsafe me but that honour)       180
    I'le be the first shall scale those feeble walls,
    and raze yon loftie turretts to the ground,
    or dye in the adventure.

*[handwritten: Religious war. Cf. Eng terms: 'rebellion' etc]*

DORA  Forbeare, *Aretas*;
    promise no more than thousands will beside.°       185

[152] advanch'd = advanced.
[154] dismaid = dismayed.
[155] feeld [field] = camp.
[156–7] i.e. we will order them to surrender or force them out …
[167] undanted = undaunted.
[185] i.e. promise to do no more than thousands of others would also promise to do …

We are departed from our home under
the conduct of a happy leader, to whom
as to the publique good we owe the tender°
of life, estate and fortune; for royal *Carola*,°

*[handwritten: Loyalty to Charles.]*

his just prerogatives wrested from him                                                    190
by an elected crew of shamelesse *Round-heads*,°
wherefore lets once again confirme our vow
in his defence that is most deere unto us.          *They draw [swords].*

ATHENIO  The motions good; joyne hands & hearts together.
    Now God defend this kingdome by our powers                   195
    whilst we for our gracious king and yours.

OMNES  Grant this, O Lord Amen, Amen, O Lord.       *And kisse the hilts.*

ATHENIO  The squadrons now must quarter in due order:
    *Dora* take you the charge thereof. My selfe,
    *Mineus* and *Aretas* will see if threats                              200
    or promises will best prevaile th' obdurate
    Newters to side with us.°                          *Enter a Scout.*

SCOUT  Arme Sirs, arme, arme!
    An army of well appointed *Angoleans*
    march directly hither.                                                    205

ATHENIO  [*March a farre off*] Never more joyfull newes.
    Come my hearts, cheer up, Hearken! This welcome
    sound invites your valour; be not found dismaid
    although your foes be arm'd; the most of ours°
    all naked men, ne're train'd to any seemely°                   210
    posture.

THEODORIKE  What troops will you appoint to give
    the charge?

ATHENIO  *Lentimos*, and you *Theodorike* must lead
    a partie forth; wee'l follow after                                      215
    with them we shall conceive expedient.

THEODORIKE  Shine happy starres; propitious fate direct us.
    Come, lets away, heaven will I hope protect us.       *Exeunt. Alarums.*

[188] tender = offer.
[189] Royal Carola = King Charles I.
[191] elected = with a pun on the Calvinist sense – to be chosen by God for salvation. 'Round-heads' (so-called because of their close-cropped hair) were supporters of Parliament during the English Civil War that was ongoing when the play was written.
[202] Newters = neutral citizens.
[209] the most of ours = the greatest / most powerful of our men. The sense is obscure but the lines seem to mean: our greatest men are unarmed and untrained.
[210] naked = unarmed.

*A good while after the alarums begun, enter Albinus and Celar severally,*
*their weapons drawne.*

CELAR  Whither shall we fly? Captain *Albinus*
    make hast away, or we are lost forever.                    220
    Our ranks are broken by the bloodie foe
    that, like so many cruell Tygers, rage
    and slaughter all they meet; with ruthfull groanes
    of dying men the aire is fill'd, and death
    in triumph waites upon our vanquisht forcers.          225

*[handwritten margin note: Reflects the rhetoric of English newssheets reporting on the Rebellion]*

ALBINUS  I scorne to flinch, or leave my harmelesse men
    a prey to them whose cruelty extends
    beyond the bounds of human nature.
    Of my estate they have deprived me else,°
    so most of those we have now seene lye dead         230
    then to revenge that wrong I led them forth,
    and to that end Ile stay; my life's no more,
    but lost augments the summe of their large score.°
CELAR  Our Serjeant Major hath forsooke the field.
ALBINUS  More Coward he.                                  235
CELAR  Shall we submit or yeeld?
ALBINUS  Neither; you may in that your pleasure doe.
CELAR  As you resolve so I will stand to it too.    *Enter Theodorike & Lentimos.*
THEODORIKE  See where *Albinus* stands, as if he meant
    to conquer all.                                 240
ALBINUS  Come on Traytor.
THEODORIKE  Thou lyest,
    base slave, that proud word shall cost thee deerely.
LENTIMOS  An equall match; come, man to man.
THEODORIKE  Fall backe good Sir,                       245
    doe you pursue the rest that flyes amaine.    *Exit Lentimos.*
    Have at you Sirs!

*[handwritten margin note: Cowardly action]*

*They fight. Celar flyes and Albinus is kill'd.*

THEODORIKE  Packe hence thou wretched soule; goe downe to stix,
    there learne of *Tantalus* what is't to strive°
    against the streame, for which he starves alive.    *Exit.* 250

[229] else = already.
[233] augment = to increase, but also to add dignity to (*OED*, 4). Albinus' life is no longer worth
living, but his death will 'augment' the deaths of his men.
[249] Tantalus was the mythical king of Phrygia who revealed the secrets of the Gods and, as pun-

*The body is taken off. Then enter Pitho, Berosus, Osirus, Cola and Tibernus.*

PITHO  When first this unexpected newes was brought us
    we little thought it would clime to that height,
    or that there were such tyrannie intended
    against the miserable Northerne Subjects;°
    but, since, we doe (unto our griefes) behold         255
    the sad disaster of our dearest friends.
COLA  Expect no better measure at their hands
    if their emperious pride be not abated.
PITHO  'Twill come too late I feare
OSIRUS  'Twish a fable;         260
    let damn'd *Medea* raise her spitefull charmes,°
    from the depth of th' infernall sootie caves,
    or from grim *Pluto's* court conjure a number°
    of armed furies; this horrid crew, were
    they more strong than hell is deepe, our just cause         265
    cryes at th' impartiall throane of God for aide
    to affront and keepe in awe these bold usurpers
    of our Soveraigne's power.
PITHO  Most nobly spoken.
BEROSUS  To thinke otherwise we should wrong ourselves,         270
    had we not lost our expectations
    for some private guilt, against the deity
    my cause of knowledge being sad and heavy,
    for the late army we sent forth, they say,
    received a fatall overthrow.         275
OSIRUS  Be not dismaid; thinke not the dismall sight
    of our defeated troupes shall strike us silent,
    or rent our fortunes with an odious tearme
    of Coward feare; 'tis a base deformed object,
    a scandal for posteritie to blot         280
    our fame. No my Lord, as yet my hopes hath life
    by the same president in other stout°

ishment, was condemned to stand in the Tartarus up to his chin in water, which receded when-
ever he stooped to take a drink, and with branches of fruit above him which escaped his grasp.
[254] Northerne Subjects = Protestant settlers in Ulster.
[261] Medea was a mythological princess and sorceress who helped Jason obtain the Golden Fleece
from her father Aeetes before marrying him. When Jason left her for Creusa, the daughter of King
Creon of Corinth, she took revenge by killing Creusa, Creon and her own children.
[262] Pluto is the Greek god of the Underworld (also referred to as Hades).
[282] president = precedent.

commanders: witnesse *Bellona's* darling,°
invincible *Caesar* (whose fame and valour°
did spread over the girdled orb, unto                                    285
the *Antipodes*), *Darius* & *Priam*, the°
*Macedonian* King, with infinit others°
impertinent to nominate. These potent
conquerors, I say, were subject to the like
misfortunes, yet not withstanding afterwards                             290
have been victorious. And why not wee?
BEROSUS  Our case, my Lord, is weake and desperate.
OSIRUS  For shame, cast off them looks of sadd dispaire;
     it ill beseemes your calling, time or place,
     an occasion seldome lesse needful                                   295
     without a further consultation. Come,
     let's goe immediately claspe on our coates
     of steell, and dare the traytors to their face
     whil'st I doe animate and lead up the rest
     of our decayed forces. Courage as then,                            300
     a little sparke may lighten all again.
PITHO  Since your undaunted spirit must needs forward,
     then be as prosperous as *Hannibal*°
     when he conveyed his army o're the mounting
     *Alps*, or like the sonne of *Jove*, when Giants°                  305
     impudence did invade the heavens.          *Exeunt omnes preter Cola.*
COLA  My hearts
     as good as theirs; had I equall power, Ide
     teare the fabricke of this world asunder;

[283] Bellona was the Roman goddess of war.
[284] Julius Caesar (100–44 BC), ruler of the Roman Empire.
[286] Darius (c.550–486 BC) was the king of Persia known as Darius the Great. He greatly extended the Persian Empire chiefly by invading Thrace and Macedonia, but was defeated by the Greeks in 490 BC. Priam was the aged king of Troy at the time of its siege and destruction by the Greeks. His son Hector led the Trojans and was killed by Achilles. When the city was sacked Priam himself was killed by Pyrrhus, Achilles' son.
[287] Alexander the Great was the king of Macedonia from 356 to 323 BC, and was considered the greatest conqueror of classical times.
[303] Hannibal (247–182 BC) was the legendary general who led the Carthaginians against Rome during the second Punic War. He led an army from Spain through the Alps and into Italy where he waged war for fifteen years before finally being defeated by Scipio in Zama in 2002. After fleeing first to Carthage and then to Crete, he eventually took poison to avoid being handed over to the Romans.
[305] A reference to the mythical battle between the Gods and the Giants in Olympus, and to Heracles (or Hercules), son of Jove (or Zeus) who slew the giant Alcyoneus with his arrows.

my fury like *Joves* violent thunder                                                310
should blast the earth farre worse then *Phaeton*°
in his heedles course. What would I not have done,
what Kingdomes ransackt till I had my will
of these on whom I ground my hatred still.                        *Exit.*

*Potentially treasonous rhetoric* [handwritten]

*Enter Athenio, Mineus, Aretas and Dora. They take their seates.*

ATHENIO  To satisfy the nice conceit of those                      315
    who judge our actions as their fancies are,°
    our taking armes shall to the world appeare
    a just and naturall defence in us,
    when to His Majesty ther's not the least
    conceit of any harme once meant, either                  320
    in's Royall person, Crowne or dignitie.
MINEUS  So farre we still expresse our selves my Lord,
    for in this protection is lay'd forth°
    the motives whereon wee chiefly ground this warre;
    next, with a tender care, we doe reserve                 325
    all that concernes our soveraignes right to
    the Lirendean Crowne, therein excluding
    all forraigne power, all Princes whatsoever.
ATHENIO  If such a Covenant we had not made,
    no *Caesar, Scipio, Hanniball,* nor that°                330
    worlds conqueror proud *Macedon,* were their
    expired dates renewed againe, could not,
    nay should not, subdue the gentry of *Lirenda*
    from their obedience to th' *Angolean* King:
    most firme and true since mighty *Cheapstow* did°         335
    conduct us hither.

*Cf. News pamphlets.* [handwritten]

*Emphasis on the benign motivation of the 'rebels'* [handwritten]

[311] Phaeton = the son of Helios, the Greek sun god. Helios gave in to his son's demand to ride his chariot across the sky. However Phaeton was too weak to control the horses and he rode too close to the Earth, which he would have destroyed with fire had Zeus not intervened and killed him.

[316] i.e. who judge our actions according to their prejudices ...

[323] protection = letters of protection, a document issued by the monarch which granted protection or immunity.

[330] Scipio (236–184 BC) was a Roman general and politician who defeated the Carthaginian leader Hannibal to end the second Punic War (see note to line 303).

[335] 'Cheapstow' refers to Richard de Clare, earl of Pembroke (c.1130–76) commonly known as 'Strongbow' who resided at Chepstow Castle in Wales. He was invited to Ireland by the exiled king of Leinster Diarmat Mac Murchada to assist him in the fight against his Irish enemies. In return he was offered the hand of Mac Murchada's daughter Aoife in marriage, and the succession

ARETAS  Nor doe we now intend a base revolt:
    had *Rome's* majestique throne command it so
    my humble answer saith
    give *Cæsars* due, to God thy heart and faith.°   Dual loyalty.   340
DORA  That was indeed the chiefe occasion first
    that moved us joyne with them.
ATHENIO  And will maintaine it,
    whil'st life breathes in this corps of mine.
MINEUS  And mine.   345
ARETAS  We are resolv'd to live and die together.   *Enter a Messenger.*
MESSENGER  May it please your Lordships, one *Theodorike*
    desires admittance to your Lordships presence.
ATHENIO  Goe give him entrance. Good man, his paines are
    great to draw the Commons forth.   *Exit Messenger.* 350
MINEUS  Such friends as him we need.
DORA  The more his praise.   *Enter Theodorike.*
ATHENIO  Welcome *Theodorike.*
THEODORIKE  Then know my Lords, with paines unspeakable
    I've drawne together of mine my neere allyes,   355
    their servants, friends and tenants: a thousand
    able men at *Rufus* quarters in a fit
    readiness to doe you service, when further
    know, our scouts for certain doe report, that
    fifteen hundred desperate bloodie rogues,   360
    under the command of Sir *Daretas*, at°   Scottish forces
    *Medra* haven are landed; beside one°   in the North.
    Collonell *Crambich* (a branch of the cursed
    tribe in Pickland) is trusted with the leading°
    of a thousand chosen men, all Citizens,   365

to the kingdom of Leinster. The accession of Strongbow marked the beginning of 'Old English'
rule in Ireland.

[340] See Matthew 22:21. The biblical text was often invoked by Catholics to justify their dual loyalty to Rome and to their Protestant sovereign.

[350] Commons = common people.

[361] Daretas may refer to Robert Munro (d. 1675?), major-general of the Scottish army that was
sent to Ulster to fight alongside the Protestant settlers against the Catholic insurgents. He arrived
in Carrickfergus in April 1642, and soon cleared County Down of rebels in a campaign that was
marked by indiscriminate violence against the Catholic population. See Appendix.

[362] Medra haven = unidentified.

[364–5] 'Collonel Crambich' refers to Colonel Crawford, one of the commanders of Robert
Munro's Scottish troops in Ulster. 'Pickland' = Pictland, the area of Scotland, north of the Firth
of Forth, formerly inhabited by the Picts. See Appendix.

with whom, by true intelligence, Sir *Carola*
intends t'expulse us from our native dwellings
with such a savage spleen, men, women, infants
on their mothers pape are vowed to be kild.°

*Similar to Angolean's
claims of atrocity
l. 220-225.*

ATHENIO  That project crusheth all. Notwithstanding,     370
    cosen and Collonell (a title not worth
    the least of thy applauded meritts),
    returne with such small forces as you have;
    give *Cola* a manfull skermish, and we
    shall speedily unto your aide.     375
THEODORIKE  To my
    griefe I speake it: the campe hath scarce a dozen
    pound of powder.
ARETAS  Heaven will strengthen thee.    *— fuel claims of Providence*
ATHENIO  Here take this sword, and use't against our foes.     380
THEODORIKE  Upon their carcasses Ile spare no blowes.
    Farewell my Lords, *Theodorike* will goe
    expose his fate against your powerfull foe.     *Exit.*

*Enter Florilla, Dulis, Pulchrina and Ellenora.*

ELLENORA  Yonder they are Madam.
DULIS  My thinkes they lacke     385
    them pleasant smiles of mirth, that like so many
    radiant beames of Sol gave comfort to
    the gloomy shade of our disquiet thoughts.
FLORILLA  Why therefore we doe now presume this visit,
    hoping we may at least disperse them cares     390
    that we suspect doth seize them unawares.
DORA  Behold my Lords, who comes?
FLORILLA  We are discover'd.
    Health to your Lorships.     *They rise.*
ATHENIO  Welcome faire Ladyes all.     395
PULCHRINA  Must we demande your licence to entrude?
ATHENIO  'Twere needlesse; your beauties are sufficient
    to claime a greater favour.
DULIS  Sir, you know
    'tis the desire of love fond women doe     400
    so much regard that, overcome with joy,
    you men esteemes it as a needlesse toy,

[369] pape = pap / breast.

and may perhaps our kindnesse now expresse
in the harsh language of ungratefulnesse.
ATHENIO  Your will my deere.                                         405
DULIS  Is only to be merry this new yeere,
    for Christmas being now well neere expir'd
    without the comfort of your usuall mirth,
    what joy have we? What sorrowes can prevent
    when in your looks the mappe of discontent?                  410
MINEUS  It lyes beyond the reach of female wit
    to sound the cause that doth occasion it.
DULIS  Howsoever some short time wee'l borrow
    to curb the mischiefe of a sudden sorrow.
FLORILLA  Our musicke hath of late unto them given         415
    a song penn'd by a friend that doth protest
    he loves this Nation deerely, in whose brest
    such deepe affection by their kindnesse came
    that he doth honour and respect the name.
ATHENIO  This makes you to affect it so.                          420
DULIS  Love bindes us to it.
FLORILLA  Will you be pleased to heare it then?
ATHENIO  Yes, and with thanks too.

## THE SONG

*Come away, O Come away,*
*Couragious youths, O doe not stay,*                              425
*Now's the time, brave Mars will prove*
*More powerfull than the god of love.*
    *Cast your Venus sports away,*
*Valour brooks not long delay,*
*Gods themselves are up in armes*                                430
*To protect you from all harmes.*
    *He that honour thinkes to gaine,*
*Feares no danger, woe or paine,*
*Death's grim looke or bloodie scarre*
*Makes the minde more noble farre.*                              435
    *Then make hast, O doe not stay,*
*Dallie not the time away,*
*If you meane for to persevere,*
*Now's the time, O now, or never.*

DULIS  How like you this?                                              440
MINEUS  A perfect good one, Ladie.
FLORILLA  Seeing the Poets fancie hath pleas'd you thus,
  wee crave the like respect, which granted us,
  shall not divert you long from them affaires
  whereto wee see you are enclin'd to most.            445
  How like you of a dance my Lords?
MINEUS  Fairest beautie,
  none dares denie when you expresse the law
  that keepes offending lovers most in awe.
FLORILLA  It merits not this complement; your love            450
  in this is that which we desire to prove.
  Some musicke there.

*Musicke, and the Lords and Ladyes dance.*

ATHENIO  Believe me this was neatly done.
MINEUS  And gave us much contentment.
DORA  Ladies, a banquet                                              455
  after this to entertaine our Noble friends.
FLORILLA  If that small worth you thinke will please your friend,
  leade on the way my Lords, and wee'l attend.

*Exeunt omnes preter Ellenora.*

ELLENORA  Goe, goe spend the remnant of your happy dayes
  whil'st I with silent grief doe vent my thoughts,     460
  thoughts able to dismay a minde most resolute
  if what a maidens braine conceives will take
  effect. Our woefull houres are posting on;
  we may be confident *Angolias* furie,
  arm'd with a mortall hatreds ready bent                465
  to mischiefs, void of pittie, with pretence
  this cruell rage is in their owne defence,
  least we who have been still as slaves to them
  should now endeavour to regaine our owne
  religion, lawes and liberty; this, O this              470
  it feares me will produce more inhuman
  acts than ever brutish *Nero* did invent.°

[472] Nero (AD 37–68) was Emperor of Rome and infamous for his cruelty.

Oh, oh, silly heart, why doest thou figure forth
so strange a forme? Silence no more, no more;
let not the aire be private to thy grief,°                    475
fearing some fatall starre approves thy speech
propheticall, and make these thoughts in fact
a mournfull Chorus to the following act.                    *Exit.*

[475] i.e. let not the air be privy to ...

## ACT II

*Enter Athenio, Mineus, Aretas, Dora, Theodorike and Lentimos. Beat a march.*

ATHENIO  This day (deere friends and kinsmen) we must behave
    our selves like brave courageous *Lirendeans*,
    not regarding the politique stratagems
    of *Cola*, wherein he thinks to find us
    in a foule disorder, his Machavillian°              5
    plots ne're so privately contrived but heaven,
    you see, doth send us timely notice, wherefore
    wee'll expect him with spirits altogether
    void of feare; what though wee are not so well
    arm'd as he, nor furnisht with that plentie          10
    of ammunition, the justnesse of our cause
    will shield us from that spitefull fury of his
    invading power. Be sensible of your wrongs;°
    (the infamous disgrace without respect
    of birth or person); how odious the name         15
    of Catholique hath ever been unto them!
    A hatred there's by inheritance, the losse
    of your estates by a thousand damn'd inventions,°
    beside innumerable edicts against Religion.
    These torments were not held sufficient         20
    in respect we somewhat yet possesse of this
    our native soile, wherefore they have contriv'd
    the last and worst of evils, to raze us from
    the world, no, nor leave so much as one alive
    to encrease the memory of us hereafter         25
    (a grudge sutable to hells blacke purposes.)
    Reflect, I pray, how neere it doth concerne
    us then to venture our lives and fortunes
    in a noble vertuous way that truly tends
    to the safety of your wives, children and friends.    30
    Admit gentleman of the worst may happen;
    what an they breake on ours: 'tis no dishonor,°

[5] i.e. Machiavellian.
[13] i.e. the wrong you have suffered …
[18] A raft of discriminatory legislation had been passed in the English Parliament to deprive Catholics of their land and curtail their rights. In March 1642 the Adventurers' act confiscated the land of Irish rebels and allocated it to those who contributed to the military effort against them.
[32] an = if.

neither our reputations blemisht in't
when th' advantage of armes and numbers theirs.
May not fortune as well grace our desires                    35
when all her motions are uncertaine? Should wee
defeate them now, the world would speake our praise.    — looks beyond
Come, let's resolve to doe them more annoy                 Britain to Europe.
than *Agamemnon* in the warres of *Troy*.°
LENTIMOS  The grave and learned eloquence of Roman         40
    Orators (noble Colonell) could not
    more perfect a description give of those
    insufferable injuryes which captivated
    our hearts in chaines of ice, that must again
    (perforce) dissolve in flames of just revenge.         45
THEODORIKE  Our enemies too neare approach, else we could
    enlarge the subject of this conference
    with as many materiall circumstances,         — grievances are endless.
    which for the present we abbreviate to prosecute
    our right. Leade on Sir, bravely guide the way;        50
    heaven will, I hope, grant this our happy day.    *Exeunt. Alarums.*

*Soon after the alarums begun, enter Cola, his weapon drawne.*

COLA  Was ever seene or heard such bold, audacious
    rogues that dares upbraid my fury? Have not I,
    to their confused shame and losse, caused many
    townes and villages to be destroyed in                 55
    dreadful flames, themselves like dismall fugitives
    compeld to flye? And yet they dare affront me still!
    O impudence, that with extracted villanie
    deserves a totall ruin, thy harme I seeke,
    and longe to glorie in soe good an action.             60
    Motives sufficient doth enduce me to it:         Confirms Athenio's
    to hang, to racke, to kill, to burne, to spoile,       accusation.
    untill I make this land a barren soile.             *Exit.*

*Alarums. Enter Athenio and Lentimos severally, their weapons drawne.*

LENTIMOS  Fly Cosen fly, ther's no hope of safety else.
    Notwithstanding a stout resistance, our men             65

[39] Agamemnon was the leader of the Greek forces during the Trojan war. He was murdered by
his wife Clytemnestra and her lover Achilles.

(affrighted with the unusuall sight of blood
and slaughter) are foully broken on, routed
by a number crueller than famisht°
lions in th' Arabian desert. *Cola*
like a demi-divell or Canniball, cryes                                        70
    out: kill, kill, spare neither man, woman, child;
    regard not age or sex, downe, downe with them all!
ATHENIO  For Christ his passion doe you once more oppose
    his furie. Make good the trench whilst I perswade°
    our timorous men to face about.                    *Exit Len[timos.]*  75

            *As Athenio would depart, enter Celar.*

CELAR  Stand traitor;
    perfidious traytor, stand!
ATHENIO  Thy foe,
    a loyall subject, and prove it so; on your guard Sir!        *They fight.*

*Celar is kild [and] Athenio departs. Then Cola enters with Tibernus and Souldiers.*

COLA  *Tibernus*, charge *Crambich* post unto the bridge°          80
    where the most number of the villens are
    in strife to passe; let not a mothers child
    escape, but see due execution on them all.
TIBERNUS  Your will shall be observ'd effectually.        *Exit Tiber[nus]*.

            *[Cola] spies Celar kil'd.*

COLA  What stout *Celar* kil'd? O damn'd bewitching fate.          85
    Beare hence this body, then after take the
    pillage of the towne for your good service.              *Exeunt.*

                *Enter Belfrida.*

BELFRIDA  Now as I live its like to prove a mad world,
    a desperate time with our Citizens;
    an' it continue thus, where they did breake                  90
    by dozens heretofore, we shall have hundreds
    now at a light rate i'faith. Such pretty

[68] number = a number of men.
[74] Make good = improve or defend.

shifts and sleights are so cunningly contrived
these days under a pretence of safetie, as
shutting shops, packing up goods and sent the 95
Lord knows whither. Coine, jewels, plate, household-stuffe,
every thing vanisheth like superfluous
clouds to the vast center of the hollow earth.
My countreymen are styled to discontented
gentlemen; well, if e're I did intend 100
to make a fortune, now's the time to stirre
my selfe, a fitter opportunitie
will never offer my acceptance; ha,
the mischiefes out, I shall be reputed so,
a prime promoter. Tush! A blast of breath 105
no sooner blowne than gone. Honesty cannot
thrive at all times; the proverb sayes, he must
needs dye a begger that is knowne too just,
wherefore I will scrue up my wits to the
full height of knavery, whereby I may 110
demurely insinuate my selfe with the
good liking of Sir *Carola*, whom no sooner's
made acquainted with my facultie, but
heapes of honour will fall on me straight, with
good Sir, sweet Sir, as I doe passe them by: 115
helpe me, sayes one, I am condemn'd to dye,
there's twentie peeces; another calls, kinde Sir,
remember my petition you preferred,° 
here's expedition for it; thus, 'twixt em all,
I'me sure to rise whosoever chance to fall. *Enter Tibernus.* 120
Here comes the only man in credit with
Sir *Carola*. Prosperitie waite on
your noble selfe, *Tibernus.*
TIBERNUS  Thanks, honest friend.
BELFRIDA  I have been since these warres desirous, Sir, 125
to doe the governor some speciall service,
but, since, could not the happiness to impart
what I am sure will please and profit him.
TIBERNUS  Relate thy minde to me, and thou shalt have
a fit reward. 130
BELFRIDA  To place my low fortunes
on the pyramide of his bounty were

[80] post = to go quickly.
[118–9] i.e. remember my request you helped bring about – here is payment for it …

a praise befitting the worthy motions
of a generous soule. This did enduce
my zealous love to shew the subtill prankes                    135
of some penurious Citizens, that lately
closed up in a wall at least a thousand
pound in plate and cash.
TIBERNUS  [*Aside*] There's some strong hopes in this.
BELFRIDA  I'le bring you likewise to each papist house,        140
    where privately are kept, trunks wholly loaden
    of rich apparel, coine, jewells, rings, bracelets,
    patents of the rebells lands.°
TIBERNUS  That especially!
BELFRIDA  What can you thinke or name best needfull for         145
    your use, but I will straight discover?
TIBERNUS  Surely
    thou canst not misse a brave preferment.°
BELFRIDA  Under pretence of being bred a Papist,
    I shall, without the least thought of suspicion,           150
    conduct your guard where Priests in secret are°
    lockt up at Masse, or in the night as they
    abroad doe creeping passe the street; moreover,
    Sir, if the army be in want, or that
    of force you aske assistance from the townsmen              155
    where some may better spare more gold than others,
    let me alone to search the difference
    of those mens fidelitie: how able, willing,
    really affected. Papist above Protestant,
    I am expert in all.                                          160
TIBERNUS  [*Aside*] Gracelesse villen
    that cares not to betray his deerest friends
    to them, wotes not after he were hang'd.°
    I must dissemble with the knave a while
    for my owne end. Now trusty friend make good                165
    what thou hast said, and blesse this house for ever.
BELFRIDA  Your constant servant, I will still persevere.        *Exeunt.*

---

[143] patents = land deeds.
[148] i.e. thou can not fail to be rewarded with a fine promotion / advancement.
[151–2] In 1585 Elizabeth I passed an act that made it high treason for any Jesuit or seminary priest
to be found within the realm, and a felony for anyone to harbour them.
[163] i.e. he does not know that afterwards he will be hanged …

*Enter Athenio, Mineus, Aretas, Dora and Cephalon.*

MINEUS  Brother *Athenio*.
ATHENIO  What sayes our deere brother?
MINEUS  Have you not hard of the late proclamation?°                         170
ATHENIO  Yes Noble Brother, I perused it over:
   the treacherous modell of a rude invention.    ✳
    *Pitho* would thousands give for all our heads.
CEPHALON  No, there's a milder since, full of Clemencie:
    a generall pardon.                                                    175
ATHENIO  To whom?
CEPHALON  Them will submit to the Lords Justices.
ATHENIO  On what conditions?
MINEUS  Perverse crueltie?
ARETAS  Perpetuall slavery?                                                   180
DORA  And mortall hatred?
ATHENIO  Very true; these are the glorious titles
    every faint hearted native will revolt
    shall have, which from my heart I wish it him;
    but to explaine my owne particular185
    intention may to the wise perhaps seeme
    needles; yet he that loves his Country, or°
    will professe the Characters of Catholique,
    in's heart take notice oft: our quarrell is
    religious, in maintenance whereof we                                190
    are already sworne without equivocation,
    and e're I violate that sacred oath,
    a thousand deaths shall one by one invade me;
    if floods of misery, I'le wade them o're,
    and from its raging streames regaine the shore                      195
    of bless'd fidelitie.
DORA  May all the world
    example take by this Lord's goodnesse.
CEPHALON  Under favour,
    'twere a folly, a most profound madnes                              200
    to seeke our certaine ruin by deniall
    of a benefit so conveniently
    proffer'd, when our wants at the most extreme.
    Both day and night I posted hence the kingdome

[170] hard = heard.
[187] needles =needless.

over, all parts my wandring thoughts conceived 205
might best supply our wants, did I returne
ought but the fruitlesse labour of a needfull
journey; can *Stelem* now your foes encrease,
make up two thousand compleat armes in field?
Your Lordships knows this is no fable. 210
ARETAS  Good Sir forbeare, the matter's past dispute.

*Enter a Messenger.*

MESSENGER  An please your excellence, severall gentlemen
of the Countie are newly come in post,
with some strange newes, it's feared by their sad looks.   *Exit Mess[enger].*
ATHENIO  Direct 'em hither; some stragling troupers 215
that for pillage scout abroad, makes false
alarums to afright the Countrey thus.   *Enter Theodorike.*
*Theodorike*, your newes? What, sad upon't?
THEODORIKE  *Osirus*,
with a powerfull army gather'd from all parts, 220
at least consisting of eight thousand foote
and horse, march hitherward, burning of townes,
distroying Castles faire; all to the sword goes
that his army meets, and doth intend (the which
good God forbid) to make a fatall conquest 225
of this land.
ARETAS  What strange, dishonest, base device
is this, to publish to the world a generall
pardon, before which time appointed is expir'd,
poore harmelesse subjects kil'd, the kingdome fir'd. 230
O faithlesse, wicked Crueltie!

*Enter Lentimos.*

LENTIMOS  Shift for your selves in hast,
for here will soone arrive more sullen spyes
than *Mercury* did charme in *Argo's* eyes.°

[234] Argo = Argus: in Greek mythology a monster with one hundred eyes whom the goddess
Hera used as a watchman to guard her priestess Io from the attentions of her husband Zeus. How-
ever Zeus sent Hermes (in Roman mythology, Mercury) to put Argus to sleep with his flute.
Hermes then killed Argus whereupon the monster's eyes were said to have been transferred by
Hera to the markings on a peacock's tail.

Good my Lords, dispatch; one minutes stay too long             235
  may yeeld you prisoners to untimely ends.
ATHENIO  Deare friends, we now resemble one at point
  of death, that must perforce forsake what he
  most deerely loved; life, wealth, faire possessions,
  pleasures content exchanged to sad expressions,             240
  wife laments, children their parents moane,
  each hath occasion then to sigh and groane.
  So we, distressed we, must oft among
  their dolefull ditties tune a mournefull song.
CEPHALON  [*Aside*] Let them whose will stand out, I will submit°    245
  to great *Osirus* cause its held most fit.                 *Exeunt.*


*A march is beaten, then enter Osirus, Tygranes and Tibernus.*


OSIRUS  Now through the power and helpe of heaven we are
  in safe possession of their strongest holts.°
  The foe not able to withstand our warlike
  troupes are fled, like men full of dispaire, griefe,        250
  regardlesse furie that we are thus strong,
  themselves pursued with terror of the times,
  and fearefull shadowes of base acted crimes;
  wherefore we must then cheerfully advance,
  not doubting but we truly shall e're long,                 255
  revenge sufficiently th' *Angoleans* wrong.
TYGRANES  You speake Sir, like your selfe, full of maturitie,
  the hopefull line that guides my confidence°
  from the most intricate labyrinth of dispaire,
  when *Adrohna* was at point to perish,                     260
  and plast the issue of a farre event
  on more than mortall comfort; that proposeth
  to the wicked vice, mischiefes, paines unspeakable,
  joyn'd with the grim aspect of blood and terror,
  more deserving plagues than wilful Egypt°                  265

[245] whose = who.
[248] holts = strongholds.
[257–62] The following five lines may be paraphrased: your mature wisdom is like a cord of hope that guides my confidence out from that labryinth of despair, when Adrohna was about to perish, and places (trusts) the outcome of future events to more than human (i.e. to divine) comfort (i.e. strength) …
[265–7] In the Old Testament the Egyptian Pharaoh refused to release the Israelites from slavery and was punished by God who visited ten plagues on his country. See Exodus 7–12.

        felt when her miseries were at the height
        of all extremes.
TIBERNUS  It needs must follow so,
        for in all parts they are environ'd with°
        severe Commanders, famous for their valour:          270
        your Excellence in *Stelem* and for the
        adjacent Provinces, men of knowne integritie.
OSIRUS  It is our chiefest comfort they goe on
        as prosperous as faire *Bellona's* darlings°
        when the gods were threatened by a multitude      275
        of foolish mortalls.
TYGRANES  But none with that Celeritie°
        like yours, which farre transcend theirs, went before,
        as Sol doth Luna's spangled Orb, or some
        bright starre when sable clouds doth vaile the skie.    280
OSIRUS  'Tis the noblest of your thoughts are pleased, my Lord,
        to speake our commendations greater than
        desert can warrant so much goodness.°
TIBERNUS  It cannot be denyed; your prosperous fate, fame,
        hath divulged it to the spacious world with doubled   285
        echoes of immortall praise, which makes *Angolia*
        to esteeme your actions the glory of her
        Northerne Clime.
OSIRUS  Believe me gentlemen,
        this will impaire your ripe judgement much; what    290
        tidings bring you from the Campe, my friend?    *Enter First Post.*
I POST  To know your Lordships pleasure concerning a
        prisoner that immediately is taken.
OSIRUS  How, a gentleman of quality?
I POST  He names                     295
        himselfe Lieutenant Collonell *Rufus*,
        a *Scot* by birth, a Papist by profession.
OSIRUS  Let him be forthwith sent to the Lord Justices.
TIBERNUS  Behold my Lord, here comes another Post.  *Enter Second Post.*
OSIRUS  Now friend, thy newes?                    300
2 POST  That Lord *Sileus*, *Bathillus*, one *Cephalon*
        and *Sisenna*, with many other prime

[269] environ'd = encircled.
[274] Bellona's darlings = the minions of Bellona, the Roman goddess of war. Cf. Shakespeare,
*Macbeth* I. II. 76.
[277] Celeritie = speed / swiftness.
[283] desert = merit / worthiness.

    gentlemen are joyntly come to the Campe
    in hope of a free pardon.
TYGRANES  A gibbet°                                  305
    fitts them better, good my Lord.
OSIRUS  Patience kinde Sir, when time and place will serve
    each one may justly have what he deserve;
    till then remit your censure.    — *speaks caution*
2 POST  How will your Lordship have them be disposed of?    310
OSIRUS  With a strong Convay, guard them presently°
    unto the Castle.
2 POST  It shall be duely done.               *Exeunt Posts.*
OSIRUS  Now we may say, Heaven favours us.
TYGRANES  Nothing                             315
    more certaine Sir, yet I must aske a boone.°
OSIRUS  'Tis granted, were it my estate, *Tygranes.*
TYGRANES  No more than two full Regiments of foote,
    a troope or so of horse to augment my former
    forces, with whom I meane to wast the Kingdome    320
    over, chiefly the Northerne quarter, where
    most my indignations bent, until I pull
    from those bold conspirators unsanctioned browes
    the wreath of honour, and force them to repent,
    crye, curse the houre that e're they urg'd *Angolias*    325
    warlike power.
OSIRUS  There needs no language to excite
    thy valour, nor distrust but thou maist soone
    accomplish that pleasing service both to
    God and man; come then make choice thy selfe of    330
    them resolved hearts fit to waite on so brave a leader.
    Then you for *Vistrand,* we *Stelem,* claspe hands;°
    when Martiall men thus knit, their partie stands.    *Exeunt.*

            *Enter Tibernus and Souldiers. Alarums.*

SOLDIERS  They call for quarter, and will yeeld the Castle
    if we grant it them.                         335
TIBERNUS  Goe, say they shall have it;
    promise whatever they will demand until

[305] gibbet = gallows.
[311] convay = convoy, i.e. a military or armed escort; presently = immediately.
[316] boone = favour.
[332] Vistrand = unidentified.

we gaine this place of strength; our losse is much
already. When that is done, gentlemen
and brother souldiers, their lives shall be at                              340
each of your disposals, as our poore countreymen
hath been at theirs.

1 SOULDIER  Wee'll brush their gutts, I'faith.

TIBERNUS  You were but fools and cowards else to thinke
the contrary; when heaven cryes vengeance on                               345
their sinfull heads, nature binds you effect it,
were there no more provoking motions but
the slaughter of your fellow souldiers here.

1 SOULDIER  He speaks like a true zealous Protestant.

2 SOULDIER  His words enflames my heart.                                   350

3 SOULDIER  Z'blood mine's so too.

4 SOULDIER  And mine is full resolved with this stiffe blade,
to goare the traytors throates.

1 SOULDIER  My sword likewise.                    *They draw severally.*

2 SOULDIER  Mine shall not sleepe when yours is drawn.                     355

3 SOULDIER  This is as quickly drawne too.

4 SOULDIER  But this did pretty well, and shall againe
augment the number of our foes that's slaine.

TIBERNUS  I must of force be absent now they yeld,
least your pretence of being ignorant                                      360
I granted quarter might spoile the jest; you
know your charge?

1 SOULDIER  You need not doubt, we doe. Stand, *Enter men, women and children.*
where would these traytors goe?

MAN  Where God will guide us best.                                         365

4 SOULDIER  Where the divell shall your wretched soules molest?

MAN  Hold, we had quarter promist us.

1 SOULDIER  Believe
him not, he lyes; kill, kill, let not a bastards
brat of the unhappy brood escape your hands!        *They are kild.* 370

2 SOULDIER  Looke, yonder turns a score, lets follow, follow.    *Exeunt.*

*Enter Theodorike.*

THEODORIKE  Heaven grant they perish in the world to come,
that were the foule actors of this brutish Tragedie;
deere friends and Countreymen, blame not my love,°

[374] Cf. Shakespeare, *Julius Caesar* III. II. 74–5.

[ 71 ]

if I bestow the attribute of Martirs on yee;                              375
Martyrs, O Martyrs truly with good reason too,
since for your faith you sufferd thus; live then
blest soules securely in eternall rest,
whil'st we lament your too untimely losse.
Oh that my wishes could an army raise                                     380
for this poore kingdoms safetie, whereby such
crueltie might be no more extended;
but oh, oh, these, these wishes are in vaine
when fire and sword beyond controlle doth raigne.
*Lirenda*, poore *Lirenda* now farewell,                                  385
farewell thy former pompe, all's turn'd to griefe,
attired in crimson robes of bloodie death
that none but heavens compassive motions can
subdue; cease then, O cease impatient griefe,
when God is pleased we may expect reliefe;                                390
mean time these breathlesse corps me think doe crave
that tribute which we all bring to the grave.                    *Exit.*

*The bodies are taken off.*

[ 72 ]

## ACT III

*Enter Cola in a fury.*

COLA  Plague choake him for a gracelesse villen! Not
    a minutes ease my restlesse fancie had,
    since first I understood my dismall fate;
    ha, is this your prophecie, good man halter?°
    Is this my fortune? [*He reads*] *Sir, you will be lost*         5
    *in this warre, by the hands of one you least*
    *suspect, before you shall returne againe.*
    Must my labour, my zealous labour be
    requited with a death I most abhorre?
    Not that I feare grim death, base conjurer,         10
    but that a *Lirendean* slave should vanquish
    me, and glorie in my overthrow, O, O,
    O, damn'd divells incarnate! If I die, I must!
    My life shall cost ten thousand lives accurst.     *Enter Tibernus.*
TIBERNUS  There's at least a score of arch traitors sent to     15
    towne, whereof one *Cephalon.*
COLA  Ha, *Brukill* I hope.°
TIBERNUS  The very same.
COLA  God's blessing on thy heart
    for this good newes; a very rogue in graine.°     20
TIBERNUS  There is another old Commander whom
    they did call Lieutenant Collonell *Rufus*; one
    can disclose more than a hundred more.°
COLA  I'le scrue
    it out of his old bones i'faith. Good *Tibernus,*     25
    fetch them hither.
TIBERNUS  Them all?
COLA  No, none but that paire
    of cunning rogues; desire the Constable
    to yoake the rest, they cannot be secure     30
    enough, but these shall to the racke without redemption. *Exit Tibernus.*

*Enter Tibernus, Cephalon, Rufus and Soldiers.*

[4] halter = hangman.
[17] Brukill = Kilbrew. Cephalon represents Sir Patrick Barnewall of Kilbrew. See Appendix.
[20] in grain = inveterate.
[23] disclose = give information on.

TIBERNUS  Cleare the way there for the prisoners, ho!
COLA  Are you there Sirs? Have you brought *Magna Charta*°
    to reprive you from the gollowes? Ha!°
CEPHALON  No,                                                   35
    His Majesty's more gracious.
COLA  What, what, to
    pardon a rable of disloyall Cut-throates,
    a nimble actor of this bold Commotion?
CEPHALON  I never was.                                  40
COLA  I say thou lyest, traytor,
    and sate in chiefe commission.°
CEPHALON  Never in my life.
COLA  Better confesse.
CEPHALON  What I did not?                               45
COLA  The racke shall force thee then.
CEPHALON  Mercy, great Sir, supports his royall throne
    from whence your glories are derived, and is
    th' admired Emblem of heroicall vertue
    disperst throughout the world, wherein his highnesse    50
    like a prince composed of goodness, would not
    his subjects ruin, but rather have his
    mercy eminent as himselfe is good.
COLA  Rugh curres, now y'are glad to fawne when hetherto
    'twas lofty bragges yee stood on; a treacherie    55
    I'le trample into dust, and make you know,
    before we part, what homage you doe owe.
RUFUS  Sir, for my selfe thus much I will confesse,
    not that I feare thy racke or tortures *Cola*,
    for why they shall no more than what I freely    60
    speake; I was indeed employed by the state
    of *Lirenda*, poore discontented *Lirenda*,
    to make knowne their woefull grievance to his
    Sacred Majestie, which had he knowne, doubtlesse

[33] Magna Carta was the charter obtained from King John in 1215 which guaranteed personal and political liberty for English subjects. Whether or not Magna Carta applied in Ireland was a question much disputed during the period: the lawyer Patrick Darcy (Dora) accused the former lord deputy of Ireland Thomas Wentworth of riding roughshod over the 'Common Lawes' that governed Irish subjects in the latter's trial for treason in 1641. Darcy's arguments were subsequently printed for the confederation. See Introduction.
[34] gollowes = gallows.
[42] i.e. as a lord justice.

his royall soule would grieve to heare th' unheard of          65
    crueltie thy squadrons exercise.
COLA  I tell thee, doting traytor, they are justly
    serv'd.
RUFUS  How traytor?
COLA  I traytor, to thy face I speake it.°          70
RUFUS  Even to thy selfe I doe returne the same.
COLA  How captious they thwart me with insulting
    language; leade them to execution straight.
TIBERNUS  First use the racke.
COLA  He dyes.          75
TIBERNUS  Let me beseech you Sir.
COLA  At thy request it shall be so.
TIBERNUS  The racke sirs, ho!

*The Soldiers fetch in the racke.*

RUFUS  Before that engine of inveterate
    malice comes, vouchsafe me hearing, I claime          80
    a double priviledge: first the benefit
    of your late printed Proclamation;
    *Osirus* promise next I should have quarter,
    such as became a martiall man to have,
    which now we humbly offer your acceptance.          85
COLA  Dissembling Crocodile, thy hidden spleene
    shall not corrupt justice by invective
    flattery; no, vipers, no, a world of
    tortures are more requisite.
CEPHALON  Let Mercy          90
    mitigate your rage.
COLA  Presume to speake againe,
    and by my soveraignes hand you both shall hang.
RUFUS  That were an act like thy selfe.
TIBERNUS  Come sirs you must unloose with expedition.          95
CEPHALON  Is that the recompence of our submission?
    Will neither honour, faith nor pittie move thee?
COLA  He stirres my choler; will none obey my will?
    I'le teare each limme my selfe asunder, unlesse
    with speed he suffer.          100
TIBERNUS  Do not provoke him Sir.
CEPHALON  Heaven grant us patience then.

[70] I = Aye.

[ 75 ]

*Cephalon is layd on the racke and drawne.*

COLA A standish Sirs,°
    take now th' examination as he speakes it.
CEPHALON Hold, hold, for Christs sake hold; the torment's great!    105
COLA Did'st not thou conspire to surprise the Castle?
CEPHALON Yes, yes, I did!
COLA And went to severall parts
    of the kingdome for powder?
CEPHALON I did, I did!    110
COLA Wast not thou private to their consultations?
CEPHALON Very true!
COLA Did not you then intend to
    extirpate all th' *Angolean* Protestants,
    to disposesse our Soveraigne of his Crowne,    115
    to usurpe the government of *Lirenda*?
CEPHALON My conscience cannot accuse them so.
COLA 'Tis false thou sayest.
CEPHALON O no, no, no!
COLA Rack up the villen higher yet, till he    120
    confesse; confesse I bid thee.
CEPHALON Torments force me,
    to acknowledge what was never done.
COLA How, how?
CEPHALON I doe confesse what you demand is true.    125
COLA Write that *Tibernus*, when thy rebellious
    kinsmen and thy selfe would carouse and feast,
    you wish'd my head among you there.
CEPHALON We did.
COLA For which thou shalt a twist up higher yet.    130
CEPHALON Then as you hope for mercy, Sir, forbeare;
    my paines intollerable, oh I die!
COLA Now take him off; your turne comes next.
RUFUS In vaine
    you seek to force me Sir, since what I speake    135
    shall be through feare not truth, nor will refuse
    to answer the least syllable you aske.
COLA Expect no favour, 'tis denyed thee.
RUFUS Such
    favour mayst thou at thy last judgement finde.    140

[103] standish = inkstand.

*Rufus is laid on the racke & drawne.*

O cruell tyrant, will no remorse of
 conscience enter thy blacke soule to see
 my aged limbes thus rent with tyrannie?
TIBERNUS Better confesse than languish on the racke.
RUFUS I can no more than what unto the Councell   145
 else I did.°
COLA Higher with him; confesse in hast,
 or by great *Jove* I'le racke thy life away.
RUFUS Take it, O take my wretched life away,
 so it appease thy furie; no tongue can tell   150
 what torments I endure!
TIBERNUS He faintes an please you.
COLA Let him faint and hang too, no great matter;
 a doting, proud obdurate foole will not
 confesse; goe take them hence unto the jayle.   155
2 SOLDIER Your pleasure shall be done.
1 SOLDIER Zlid, search their pockets.
3 SOLDIER 'Twill make us swill boyes, swill boyes merily.°
2 SOLDIER Thanke me for that, good man dunse, or it should
 walke to the Constable againe.°   160
1 SOLDIER His shallow Coxcomb
 had none the wit to think on't.
3 SOLDIER However, anon
 wee'll be as joviall lads, as cup and can.°  *Exeunt.*
COLA The rest shall be used with like severitie.   165
TIBERNUS 'Twere wisely done of you.

*Enter Soldiers leading in two Countreymen.*

COLA Who have you here?
1 SOLDIER Two rogues with each a bag of salt we tooke,
 going to supply their wants abroad.
COLA You have done well   170
 to intercept the knaves;
 goe bid the Provost Marshall execute
 them presently.

[146] else = previously.
[158] swill = drink.
[160] This phrase is obscure.
[164] as cup and can = a colloquial phrase denoting constant and familiar associates.

1 SOLDIER  Come away, come an' be hang'd.

MAN  Where master?                                                          175

1 SOLDIER  To be hang'd: that's plaine English.

MAN  I trow no, for what *Agra*?°

1 SOLDIER  The gallowes will

    instruct you better; come an' be hang'd, come.          *Exeunt.*

*Enter Belfrida.*

TIBERNUS  Behold your chiefe spie is return'd Sir *Carola*:          180

    your *Argos*, your pretty tell tale *Mercury*.

BELFRIDA  First, arme your grave thoughts with attentive patience

    least what I speake might prove offensive to you;

    your foes doe daily expect from *Spaine, France*°

    and the *Low-Countryes* plentie of all fit                  185

    ornaments of warre, as powder, bullet, match,°

    musketts, petternalls, and such like, moreover°

    many valiant brave Commanders.

COLA  Hell take them first,

    a brood of most disloyall vipers, ha!                       190

    What peremptorie slave durst tell this fable?

BELFRIDA  Them who invoke your happy fates for certaine

    did approve it upon oath, and further said

    one *Dictus* went for that expected ayd.°

COLA  What, is he gone to Sea?                                       195

BELFRIDA  Yes, gone to Sea.

COLA  A blister build on thy tongue, foule serpent!

    *Tibernus*, thou lovest me.

TIBERNUS  My heart and life is yours.

COLA  Speed after, good *Tibernus*, in all post,                    200

    send forth a power to watch at every coast;

    perhaps he lurkes in hollow caves abroad

    till winde and tide doth serve, whil'st this base rascall,

    (corrupted with a golden bribe) will not

    reveale his private haunt.                                   205

BELFRIDA  Sir, if I have

    offended, pardon me.

[177] Trow = trust; *A ghrá* is Irish for 'my love' or 'dear'.
[184–5] Irish regiments were stationed in France, Spain and Spanish Flanders.
[186] match = a piece of cord impregnated with melted sulphur used as a fuse.
[187] petternalls = petronel: a large pistol.
[194] Dictus = unidentified.

COLA  By heavens I will not!
    Put him into the Provost Marshalls custodie
    till further order comes from us. *Tibernus*,            210
    charge *Amphilus* on his life to scoure the Seas,°
    and let the harvest be destroyed.
TIBERNUS  It shall.            *Exeunt.*
COLA  What Hercules can remove this mountaine
    of enraged passions from my heart? O now        215
    it nothing fitts my care to speake but thunder,
    or take into my throate the trumpe of Heaven,°
    with whose determinate blasts the winde shall°
    burst that blew his sailes aloft; and th'enraged
    Seas consume their foamy waves that will not    220
    let his vessel sinke; whereby my care might
    be disperst, void of suspicion, ascending
    from this wicked plot unseene, a poisoned
    plot sufficient to infect the world, when
    they doe shew themselves the worst of men.    *Exit.* 225

*Enter Ellenora pursued by a Soldier, his sword drawne.*

SOLDIER  Stay harlot stay, or by the heavens above,
    I'le neither spare thee for reward nor love.
ELLENORA  Pittie oh pittie friend my woefull case,
    my parents are by thee already slaine;
    what would my loathsome life availe thee then?    230
    Kinde heart relent, relent if any sparke
    of civil grace be in thee.
SOLDIER  Z'blood and wounds,
    unlesse thou yeelds me freely thy virginity
    I'le pierce thy brest with this remorselesse steele.    235
ELLENORA  I scorne thy hellish motion; hands off rude divell
    or I'le convince thee with a chast denial
    like vertues darling, faire *Susanna*.°

---

[211] Amphilus = unidentified.
[217] In the Bible the 'trumpet' call heralds the apocalypse.
[218–21] The meaning is obscure but this passage seems to mean: God's trumpet blasts (i.e. his wrath) will cause the wind that previously had 'blown' the ship's sails to 'burst' (i.e. break) them, and cause the seas to become 'enraged' and 'consume' those waves that 'will not let his vessel sinke'.
[238] In the Apocrypha Susanna was a beautiful and devout Jewish woman who was falsely accused of adultery but was saved from execution by Daniel.

SOLDIER  Here's needlesse
    fustian trow, mistris twitle twatle, what now?°          240
    Nay friske about the sinquapace, all's one;°
    thou strivest in vaine to hinder my desires;
    yeeld, yeeld speedily!
ELLENORA  Never whilst I live;
    helpe, helpe!                *Enter another Soldier.* 245
2 SOLDIER  I come to helpe away your
    maiden-head, if't not be lost already.
ELLENORA  More furies yet!
1 SOLDIER  And more, if need require.
ELLENORA  O beastly filthy lewdnesse,          250
    will no compassion move you? O kill mee,
    kill me sooner than bereave me of a
    modest fame; see these eyes dimme with distilling
    teares that never knew to weepe till this sad
    houre, yet would some pitty crave from your hard      255
    hearts. O honest friends, hearken to my griefes;
    let not your better sence be deafe unto
    the woefull plaints of a distressed maiden.
1 SOLDIER  Who hath a nimble tongue, and pratles strangely.
2 SOLDIER  And as strong as a witch.        *She struggles with them.* 260
ELLENORA  Helpe, helpe in time,
    some helpe from heaven, helpe me yee powers divine!

*Enter Theodorike.*

THEODORIKE  Me thinkes I hard not very farre from hence°
    some woefull Creatures to lament and greeve,
    crying a loud for helpe, as'twere.          265
ELLENORA  Helpe, helpe!
THEODORIKE  Some ravisht virgin did emplore my aide;
    I'le therefore search this silent desert thorow°
    until I find from whence proceeds this heavy
    dolefull crye.                270
ELLENORA  'Tis shame to use a maiden thus.

[240] fustian = ranting; trow = fancy / supposition.
[241] nay friske about = don't fuss about; sinquapace = sine qua pace = Latin for 'without your leave / permission'.
[263] hard = heard.
[268] desert thorow = deserted thoroughfare.

1 SOLDIER  Zwounds jade, talke not of shame to us.

2 SOLDIER  Stab the queane!

1 SOLDIER  Z'life that's the way; this pettish harlot will
 affront us else.            275

ELLENORA  O stay thy murdering hand;
 murder, murder!

2 SOLDIER  A shee divell by God; canst not kill her troe.°

THEODORIKE  Direct me heaven, O that in time I may
 bestow my helpe; [*He spies them*] ha, what base inhuman fray 280
 is this? I did suppose as much, when first
 her shrill laments did pierce the aire, and sent
 into my soule a deepe conceit of pittie.
 Ha! Two to one weake creature, drench in teares;
 trust me the oddes is much, and marvaile shee  285
 held out so long; well, name of God, I'le forward.
 Fly shameless villens fly, if not, by heavens
 I'le force your flight, and thus revenge her wrong. *He strikes at them.*

1 SOLDIER  Rascall, thou shalt deerely repent that blow.

THEODORIKE  Release that Ladie first, I claime her mine, 290
 if not be sure this blade's as sharpe as thine.

1 SOLDIER  We meane not Sir at your request to flinch
 as if we feared thy lofty threats; no, no,
 proud loytring scab, get thee away in time,
 or thou shalt rue the houre and curse the day,  295
 in seeking to deprive us of our pray.°

THEODORIKE  Untie her speedily base pilfring rogues,
 or by them powers above, youle soon repent
 the wrong you doe this harmelesse innocent.

ELLENORA  Rescue, O rescue Noble Sir, a virgin  300
 ready to be deprived of such a treasure,
 once lost, the world cannot repaire againe.

THEODORIKE  Faire beautie be of comfort, I'le fight for thee.
 Come ruffians come, come quench your bloodie thirst,
 my heart's the fountaine drinke, drinke till y'are burst; 305
 if your insatiate lust be not yet coole,
 I'le soone extinguish that in human flame.
 Why gape you thus, whil'st valour may be had?
 Charge both at once!

1 SOLDIER  Z'life, sure the fellows mad.  310

[278] troe = here used elliptically for 'I trow' meaning 'I suppose'.
[296] pray = prey.

2 SOLDIER  Let him goe to; wee'l cure his frenzie fitts,
    or make him be more lunatike in's wits.

> *They fight; one is presently kill'd, the other soone after.*

Quarter, quarter, good Sir give me quarter.
THEODORIKE  The very same that all thy bloody tribe
    doth give my Countreymen when they submit                    315
    their fainting lives upon a faithlesse promise;
    goe, meet thy brothers soule, poore naked rogue,
    where greedie *Charon* waites to waft him ore,°
    unto great *Belzibubs* infernall shore.
    Now be at libertie; give thanks to God therefore.            320
ELLENORA  His Majesty I'le praise for evermore,         — Gives honour
    and you for this excessive kindnes thanks.                to the King
    O thankes, kinde heart, ten thousand thanks I give thee,
    wishing that heavens may shoure perpetuall°
    blessings on thee.                                           325
THEODORIKE  Deare heart, relate the legend
    of thy misfortune.
ELLENORA  Sir, my griefes would rent
    a heart of marble, were it sensible of
    them grosse abuses done (perhaps) unto                       330
    your owne deere friends as well as mine; oh *Cola*,
    that monster tyrant *Cola*, his barbarous
    command no civil thought but must lament
    to thinke ont; a Turke could not more brutish
    villaine than he, and to a kingdome                          335
    (good God) that raised both him and his from nothing.
    My aged Father, Mother, Brother, Sisters all,
    all my deere friends were basely murdered by him,
    when having notice of ther bloodie ends,
    feare lead me hither, supposing I was                        340
    free from danger; but oh, it almost proved
    a theater of rape and murder had
    not your valour ransom'd my hard fate.
    To these I did a shoure of liquid teares
    present in lieu of what they sought, but would not doe;°     345

[318] In Greek mythology Charon was the old man who ferried the souls of the dead across the
rivers Styx and Acheron to Hades.
[324] shour = shower.
[345] i.e. but it would not do …

[ 82 ]

when my chiefe comfort was the gods, oh they
would then transforme me like to *Niobes*,°
my griefs Ide most happy had I beene,°
then Metamorphos'd like that mournfull queene.                    *Weepes.*

THEODORIKE  Faire beautie doe not wast them Cristall streames,       350
    that to a lovers minde more precious is
    than *Mida's* wealth.°

ELLENORA  Perswade me not.

THEODORIKE  I will.

ELLENORA  Reason enjoynes me to obey your will,                      355
    with all them dutifull respects I owe
    your most accomplisht vertue.

THEODORIKE  Then you reward
    my small endeavours highly; come my faire
    prisoner, wherein more freedome we may                           360
    dispence with sullen griefe a while. Prethee,
    letts to the next adjacent garison
    and as (without selfe spraise) I late did shield°
    thee from the furie of these slaves, so under God
    I'le be thy safeguard thither, whence may proceed                365
    some kinde refreshment to poore soules in need.                  *Exeunt.*

*The bodyes are taken off. Enter foure Soldiers.*

1 SOLDIER  Come along brother Souldiers, the round, the round!

2 SOLDIER  Zlid Sirs, where is the best pillage found?

1 SOLDIER  At hangmans lane end, where market-folks
    with store of belliware of force must passe.°                    370

3 SOLDIER  Zlid my teeth waters else; there, let's goe there boys.

1 SOLDIER  Masse alls! But need never so payd in our dayes,°
    with mouldie scraps of cheese and butter with
    as many collours as the rainbow in't;

[347] In Greek mythology Niobe was the daughter of Tantalus, and mother to six children. She boasted of her superiority to the goddess Leto who had only two children, Apollo and Artemis. Her children were killed by Apollo and Artemis to punish her pride. Niobe wept for her children until turned into a column of stone.

[348] i.e. my grievances I'd render most happy had I been ...

[353] Midas was the legendary king of Phrygia who was given the gift by the god Dionysus to turn everything he touched into gold.

[363] self spraise = self praise.

[370] belliware = belly-ware, i.e. provisions.

[372] The sense is obscure but the meaning seems to be: our needs have only been met with ...

well, my heart's in hope we shall feast merrily 375
anon; let's be joviall, a fit of our
owne mirth, then to the worke my lads.
2 SOLDIER  What shall we have?
1 SOLDIER  What but Lord *Pitho's* song?
2 SOLDIER  Your voice is best; begin. 380

### THE SONG

1 SOLDIER  *Pitho is doting, we care not who knows it,*°
*The Worst is but three pence a day if we loose it,*
*For were he not from God knows whom descended,*
*He had on poore souldiers more freely expended,*
*Let us not then boyes expect from such men,* 385
*Any favour whose honour was got with the pen.*
OMNE  *Cast away care boyes, trouble not your minde,*
*For we shall be payd, when the divell is blinde.*
2 SOLDIER  *'Tis too well knowne sirs such men to get pelfe,*
*With strange devices rob the common-wealth,* 390
*By a colloging craftie kind of stealing,*°
*They are made great ones, O fie on false dealing,*
*Then let us pray boyes, for them will thus palter,*°
*May justly be serv'd in their kinde with a halter.*
OMNE  *Cast away cares boyes, etc.* 395
3 SOLDIER  *No marvaile then sirs, wee seeke after pillage,*
*In citie, suburbs, towne or countrey village,*
*When our grave statesman conceives it good pay,*
*A souldiers allowance but three pence a day,*
*Then helpe your selves boyes, O 'tweare a bravado,* 400
*If wee could but see Pitho in the strapado.*°
OMNE  *Cast away care boyes, etc.*

*Enter a Traveller.*

1 SOLDIER  Silence gentlemen, stand cleere; yonder comes
a traveller.

---

[381] doting = weak-minded / stupid.
[391] colloging [collogue] = to employ feigned flattery / to cajole.
[393] palter = to act evasively / to equivocate for treacherous ends.
[401] strapado [strappado] = a form of torture in which the victim's hands are tied behind his back
and attached to a pulley. He is then hoisted up and let down again with a jerk.

2 SOLDIER  I'le dive into his pockets straight.                                405

3 SOLDIER  His cloake is mine already.

4 SOLDIER  And if his felt°
    be worth the taking; from whence come you Sir?

TRAVELLER  Who gives authoritie to question me?

1 SOLDIER  Povertie bids us to examine you;                                410
    canst lend us money friend?

TRAVELLER  Not a pennie.

2 SOLDIER  Wilt thou bestow some on us then?       *They rifle him.*

TRAVELLER  Forbeare, forbeare.

1 SOLDIER  Wee must change cloakes.                                         415

3 SOLDIER  Your felt is good I see.

TRAVELLER  You will not deale thus shamefully I troe?°

1 SOLDIER  Gat thee gone; begone, or I will make thee goe.

TRAVELLER  With a light purse, and a heavy heart.      *Exit.*

1 SOLDIER  See, see, 'tis waightie silver O my conscience!                  420
    Well, wee'll share anon; good lucke attend us.

*Enter a Maid servant.*

Who comes next?

4 SOLDIER  A maid with something in her lappe.

1 SOLDIER  Stirre not a foote, she comes directly this way;
    what ha'st thou here sweetheart?                                     425

MAID  Nothing for you.

1 SOLDIER  What need you be so coy? 'Tis ne're the worse
    wee see't.

MAID  Not much the better neither; loe,
    'tis bread and meat my mistris sent me for                            430
    unto the market.

2 SOLDIER  Your mistris put not°
    a crum of this into her chappes, by God.

MAID  Thou louzie, filching rogue let goe my meate,
    or I will to thy captaine presently                                   435
    complaine; cannot folks passe the streets for you?

2 SOLDIER  There's thy napkin, we scorne baseness.

MAID  Baseness?
    Base rogues, what are you else?

[407] felt = hat.
[417] troe [trow] = trust.
[432] put not = will not put.

3 SOLDIER  Do'st call us rogues?                                          440
MAID.  Your actions speakes it so
2 SOLDIER  Z'life trull begon,
    or I will kicke thee home an angrie spider
    to grumble for a little victuals thus.
3 SOLDIER  Get home scold, get home!                    *They beat her off.* 445

*Enter a Gentleman.*

4 SOLDIER  A prize, a prize!
1 SOLDIER  Stand close, for if he spies us hee'll drop in
    some house or other. Save you Sir.
GENTLEMAN  And you likewise.
1 SOLDIER  Kinde Sir, regard a Souldiers want; something            450
    to drinke, your bounty Sir.
GENTLEMAN  There's twelve pence for yee.
2 SOLDIER  In earnest of a greater summe, your leave Sir.
GENTLEMAN  Keepe off, you are too forward Sirs.
1 SOLDIER  Draw if you dare,                                              455
    an thou lovest thy life starre not.°
GENTLEMAN  I am a Protestant.
2 SOLDIER  Be what you will, all's one to us sweet Sir.      *They rifle him.*
GENTLEMAN  Restore my purse, and I'le part with it freely.
2 SOLDIER  An' if we doe the King shall know it; ha, ha!             460
GENTLEMAN  I must share with mine owne.
3 SOLDIER  You looke to be beaten;
    I see that! Goe to the Councell complain;
    tell *Pitho*! An himselfe were here, I'de doe as much.
GENTLEMAN  There's no contesting with these desperate knaves.   465
                                   *Exit* [Gentleman].
1 SOLDIER  Ha ha brother, am not I a nimble lad?
3 SOLDIER  Packings and that, thou art.°
4 SOLDIER  Grammercy bully,
    how has learn'd the tricke, ant?
2 SOLDIER  Ah, to plunge into                                            470
    a well lin'd pocket; no art
    beyond it.

[456] life starre = lifestar. The line seems to refer to the belief that an individual's life is controlled
by the stars and planets.
[467] Packings = fraudulent actions / plots.

3 SOLDIER  Or to whip off a hatt or a cloake
  and a wey-wit; but say what occupation°
  likes thee best?                                                      475
4 SOLDIER  Warr's but a pedling figarie,°
  with a number of lowzie customers:
  knocks, hunger, cold, thirst, the captain's-pay, a
  disease that sore torment us, 'tis a most
  unchristian purgation; some vermin too,                                480
  la, they creepe, bite and keepes a damnable quarter
  on my shoulders, an' I could shrug them off,
  I'de ne're desire 'em againe.
2 SOLDIER  No better
  barrell better hering on us all; we can°                               485
  sing the same song to the tune of *Lachrimæ*,°
  but to the purpose.
4 SOLDIER  Faith, mine jumpes right with°
  thine, Bullie, 'tis a neate kinde of trade; we onely
  borrow from those can spare it, yet I say                              490
  'tis more gentill far than three pence a day.
1 SOLDIER  Has hit the nayle i'th'head; come shake hands,
  this day we thrive lads, tomorrow againe
  boyes; a short life and a merry, Sirs, follow
  your leader!                                                           495
  *Omnes*  O brave *Timothy*, O rare *Timothy*.          *Exeunt.*

  *Enter Tygranes and Barbazella with a guard.*

BARBAZELLA  If ere I did conspire with Cornet *Brinfort*,°
  or knew of his departure before I was
  inform'd he went, O let me ne're behold
  Sun, Moone, Starres, or any Celestiall power                          500
  that keepes due motion in their proper spheres.
TYGRANES  Perjured slut, thy compliances are yet extant,°
  whose owne confessions doe approve thy crime.

[474] a way-wit = away with it.
[476] figarie [fegary] = vagary.
[485] 'No better barrel better herring' is a proverbial phrase meaning 'never one better than the other'.
[486] 'Lachrimæ' refers to well-known melancholy tune popularized by the composer and lutenist John Dowland (1563?–1626) in *Lachrimæ* (1604), his collection of 21 pieces for the viol and lute.
[488–9] i.e. I agree with you.
[497] Cornet = A commissioned officer in a troop of cavalry who carried the colours; Brinfort = unidentified.
[502] i.e. your accomplices are still alive.

BARBAZELLA  Produce my accusers.

TYGRANES  Them gentlemen                                            505
    that now are in restraint for the same fact
    speakes thy accomplisht willingnesse.

BARBAZELLA  O no!
    Doe not cast that foule aspersion on them;
    so farre I doe presume their worth is such,        510
    that death cannot urge them expresse as much.

TYGRANES  This falsehood shall in thy blood appeare.

BARBAZELLA  Noble Sir,
    my fault as you have censured it never
    deserv'd the least of this, God knows; if innocence   515
    may pleade my cause, no soule more wrong'd than I.    *Weeps.*

TYGRANES  Them teares resemble *Synons* trecherie°
    against old *Priams Troy*, whereof 'tis said:°
    vice doth her just hate never more provoke,
    than when she vailes it under vertues cloake;        520
    discover *Brinforts* plot immediately
    or as I live I'le spare no tortures on thee.

BARBAZELLA  Enjoyne my sinne some other penance; if truth
    must not appeare t' aquit me from so foule
    a scandall, hide, O hide my loath'd face in some    525
    nastie gloomy dungeon, or hang in chaines
    until I eate the flesh that ne're offended.°
    Here then my naked brest, readie to receive
    what you will scribe thereon; my blood will serve
    instead of inke, where if you please record         530
    how willingly I suffer'd for my Lord
    and maker Christ.

TYGRANES  For lustfull treason rather,
    until thou dost confesse. I'le write in wounds
    fit characters to thy rightfull sufferance.          535

*Here shee is drawne aloft with burning matches between each finger.*

---

[517] A reference to the story of the 'Trojan Horse' found in Homer's *Odyssey*. In order to capture Troy the Greeks built a wooden horse in which they concealed their best warriors. Sinon, pretending to be a deserter, accompanied the horse to the city gates, and told the Trojans the horse was an offering to the goddess Athena and that, once inside, it would render the city impregnable. The Trojans admitted the horse and their city was taken.

[518] Priam was the king of Troy.

[527] i.e. Eucharist.

BARBAZELLA  O kill me, kill me, doe but grant that favour!
    Be no more crueller than death; feele, O feele,
    your heart's transform'd to stone; let my heart's blood
    dissolve your selfe againe, else you'le become
    the lively portraicture of tirannie.                  540
TYGRANES  Thus I expresse me yet.
BARBAZELLA  And yet I live!
TYGRANES  All the torments hell can boast of shall be
    inflicted on thee; not suddenly, no,
    but with a fretting paine vex thy desire.           545
BARBAZELLA  Thy cruell thoughts to hell's dark plagues aspire.
    Jesu Redeemer of my soule, to thee
    I must address my pittifull complaint,
    when men takes lesse remorse on contrite teares
    than Tigers doe; thou knowest, O Lord, whither°     550
    my thoughts were ever guiltie of that crime
    deserving this unheard of crueltie, but, O
    eternall wisdome, my grief cryes at thy
    watchfull eare for every; vouchsafe it may°
    abate them torments that will last for aye.        555
I SOLDIER  [*Aside*] How resolute these pettish Papists are;
    she'd sooner let her fingers burne to th' bone
    than once reveale a rebels base intention.
2 SOLDIER  Who was her sweetheart, and loved him deerely.
I SOLDIER  Mas lad, an seemes so.                  560
TYGRANES  Speake huswife, speake.
BARBAZELLA  What would you have me speake?
TYGRANES  What *Brinforts* plot was in departing hence.
BARBAZELLA  Aske me no more, I am a stranger in't.
TYGRANES  Did ever man behold such impudence?     565
    I know thou lyest.
BARBAZELLA  O be not thus incredulous.
    Jewes, Turkes, Infidells, yes Heathens too, all°
    nations doe commiserate the dolefull
    paines of them like me, nor will not urge them    570
    further once the fire exposed; but your beliefes
    more strange than theirs.

[550] whither = whether.
[554] for every = forever.
[568–71] The syntax here is ambiguous but the meaning seems to be: even Unchristian nations (Jews, Turks, Infidels and Heathens) feel compassion for prisoners and will not continue to question them after they have been tortured …

TYGRANES  Confesse, thou foolish wench confesse,
    or I will cause new match to be applied.
BARBAZELLA  Doe what you please; my God I trust will strengthen      575
    me against thy hellish furie.
TYGRANES  'Tis a folly
    to compel this slut I see; goe, take her off,
    untill some evidence comes in against her.        *Exeunt.*

## ACT IV°

*Enter Abner reading a letter, attended by two sons.*

ABNER  [*Reads*] *Unlesse you speedily repaire unto our aide,*
    *the Kingdom's lost beyond recovery.*
    O fearfull newes, newes that doth rent my heart
    to heare it.
I SON  Why noble father? You have               5
    received as desperate tydings oft before,
    yet made your thoughts contemne the worst might follow,°
    and when occasions offer'd, as bravely did
    performe it; rebuke this passion then, Sir.
2 SON  Good father doe;                10
    our joyes in your contentment.
ABNER  Fond youthes, your yet unripened yeares brookes not
    the lowring jesture of deserved sorrowes
    (how neere soever it concernes you.) Why
    your spring o'retops the Autumne of my yeares,      15
    your griefes a weather-cocke, subject to change
    at every blast of youthfull pleasure;
    but when dame nature dyes your flaxen curles
    a reverend gray, experience will confute°
    that long deluding follie. This is no          20
    common toy (like yours) to grive at; no, no,°
    peruse them mournefull lines, where if you find
    not cause of lamentation, blame me then.

*He gives the letter* [and] *they peruse it.*

I SON  Ha, *Lirenda* at point to be destroyed!
    O brother see, that countrey whence we are      25
    discended calls for some timely succour;
    nature must worke a true compassion in us.
    Father, O Father, by all that is most
    deere unto you, regard this sad complaint.        [He] *gives it back.*

[Lines 1–169 take place in Spain.]
[7] contemne =play down / underestimate. The lines seem to mean: you have never overestimated
the situation before, but have always acted bravely when occasion offered.
[19] confute = prove wrong.
[21] toy = frivolous piece of writing; grive = grieve.

ABNER  Now be your selves the judge whether we ought not          30
    pitty them, or preferre their safetie sooner
    than all the fortunes mightie *Spaine* will give us.
    Value the difference pray: here we be indeed
    accommodated with respect and honour,
    wealth sufficient for our betters, with the          35
    grace of *Spaine's* Emperiall Monarch;
    what doe we lacke? Nothing, but yet compared
    to the affection of our Countrey, not worth
    the speaking.
I SON  Weed rather forfeit what we have,          40
    than stay a minute once our friends doe crave.
ABNER  That's each of your firme resolution.
AMBO  We humbly yeeld to your mature direction.
ABNER  Goe haste to your mother and prevaile with her,
    for I must yet a while consult alone.          *Exeunt ambo.*  45

*Abner layes him on a couch and slumbers. Then enter the Queene of fates, attended by*
    *three Nymphes viz. Clotho, Lachysis and Attropos.*°

QUEEN  See where a second *Mars* lyes, *Abner* nam'd,
    faire Nymphes respect him, or you'l be all blam'd
    of too, too, coy demeanour. Musicke, some *solemne musicke*,
    musicke or harmonious spheare descend,
    descend whil'st we his vertues doe commend.          50
CLOTHO  Faire Queene, the gods are pleas'd you know we should
    appeare unto this mortall to unfold
    their divine pleasure and most sacred will,
    in heaven decreed, wherefore we must fulfil
    the promisses of their superior powers          55
    above, and as we doe esteeme him ours,
    thus I declare his fortune: in respect
    of warlike graces none shall more direct
    than his mature command, his valour too
    shall make his adversaries blush to know          60
    that from an infant heaven did him elect          *Divine providence*
    to be victorious still against their Sect.          *confirmed*
LACHYSIS  Opinion, Mistriss, sayes a silent tongue,
    consents to every thought; then I should wrong
    his happiness if I did not relate          65
    what I am sure will much augment his fate:

    heroique valour, vertue, a pregnant wit,
    are them deportments we conceive best fit
    to crowne his future actions; this wee give
    for an assurance that his fame shall live.          70
ATTROPOS  Grave Matron, from you I must needs borrow
    leave to speake in's praise; before tomorrow
    visits the world, this discontented couch
    whereon hee's stretcht, 'tshall witness and avouch
    these promis'd happines.          75
QUEEN  Y'are all content,
    wee see, to raise his fame.
CLOTHO  The gods themselves doth honour *Abner's* name.
QUEEN  Let each of you in Sonnets sound his joy,
    mixt with a dance or some conceited toy,          80
    to pleasure him withal, whil'st sleeping thus
    he may receive a happy fate from us.

## THE SONG

*Morpheus wee conjure thee hence,*°
*Goe to them gloomy shades from whence*
*All sorts of lurking mischiefes flow*          85
*Beneath th' infernall depths below,*
*Goe to Stix, Averre, or whither,*°
*Tell the gods exil'd thee thither.*
*Let no sad thought then mollest him,*
*Wet from sadnesse dispossest him,*          90
*But contrive for him fit praise*
*With length of many happy dayes,*
*So loud fame his Worth may sound*
*Through the universall round.*
*Them bloodie troupes that doth destroy*          95
*His native Ile, like wretched Troy,*
*In sad laments shall grieve to see*
*Hence forward them victorious bee,*
*O thy remorseless rage in vaine,*
*Lirenda florisheth againe.*          100

    *As the song is ended, enter Mars, Bellona, Pallas and Mercury.*

[Stage Direction] In Greek mythology Clotho, Lachesis and Atropos were the three Fates.
[83] In Greek and Roman mythology Morpheus was the god of dreams.

BELLONA  See where the stately Queene of fortune sitts,
    like *Citherea* daughter unto *Jove*,°
    to her we must addresse our best salutes:
    all haile faire Queene!
QUEEN  Welcome, deere sister.                  105
MARS  Faire Empresse, we hard your solemne notes ascend°
    up to the highest point of heavens great arch,
    from whence we come to fill an emptie spheare
    with comfort, the discontented *Lirendeans*.
MERCURY  The gods and goddesses are wholly bent     110
    to vanquish all their former discontent,
    though hetherto they seem'd not to regard 'em,
    yet notwithstanding they are now resolv'd
    henceforth to let their sorrowes be dissolved.
QUEEN  Wee knew as much good *Mercury*, and doe     115
    applaude that act, which argues them just gods;
    'tis fit we publish then, what they decreed.
    Brother *Mars*, you must furnish them with armes,
    and *Pallas* wisedome 'gainst intestine harmes,
    our selfe, and you *Bellona* in the field,     120
    will make the bloodie adverse partie yeeld
    to the stout *Lirendeans*: oft pursued
    by them unjustly almost were subdued.
    Their Sol thus long ecclipst againe must shine,
    to shew the lustre of them lamps divine     125
    that best predominate their happy fates;
    we meane them starres which on that Iland smile
    to see they shoo'd retaine their light a while
    by a darke cloudie mist that now is spent,
    and forc'd to vapour in the Orient.     130
    Therefore resolve, as we long time did since,
    with your immortall powers for to convince°
    as many armed furies as will dare
    repine at *Abners* deeds, or seeke to share°
    in them adventures wee are pleased to give     135
    a good successe unto; his fame shall live
    that once it might be said: dame fortunes wheele

[87] Averre = Averne: a French word meaning the pit of Hell.
[102] Cytherea was another name for Aphrodite, the Greek goddess of love.
[106] hard = heard.
[132] convince = overcome / vanquish.

became soone stedfast when it most did reele.
OMNES  By *Jupiter* agreed.
QUEEN  Dear sister come, take                                         140
    your seate whilest my chast Nymphes, grac't with these
    gods, doe dance.

*      They take their seats. Musicke. The Gods and Nymphes doe dance,*
*              which ended, they rise.*

QUEEN  Now your free bounties are bestowed wee see
    in each respect, as we desired shoo'd be;
    such thankefulnesse, that to your deities due,                145
    fortunes great queene doth tender each of you.
    Now gently, gently, wake him as we goe
    up to our spheares, thence view his deeds below.    *Exeunt.*

*    He is wakned with solemne Musicke and this following song:*

## THE SONG

*Hence flattring Somnus get away°*
*With thy drowsie leaden mace,*                                       150
*That which makes the brightest day*
*Blacker then a Negro's face,*
*Here's no biding for thee goe,*
*Once the Gods command it so.*
*      Rise from his tempting couch, O rise*                  155
*Couragious Abner, doe not stay,*
*Lirenda calls aloud and cryes,*
*Brave Abner come, O come away,*
*Him Victoria guardeth still,°*
*Can best assuage our present ill.*            *Abner wakes.*  160

ABNER   Is't in a dreame I saw this heavenly vision,
    or is't vaine fancies daseling on mine eyes?°
    Sure I slept sound indeed, but ne're with so much
    blest content before; a dreame it cannot be,
    a blessed inspiration rather, that yet                        165

[134] repine = to complain / to express discontent.
[149] Somnus was the god of sleep.
[159] Victoria = a figure of the goddess Victory.

possesse my thoughts with a most sweet delightfull
comfort; well, in few words I am resolved,
propitious heaven, now I emplore thy aid;
him thou'lt assist, needs not to be dismaid.                    *Exit.*

*Enter Athenio, Mineus, Aretas and Dora.*

ATHENIO 'Tis more than time wee looke to right ourselves          170
  on that foule wretch and tyrant *Cola*,
  least suddenly we forfeit for our slakenes
  the losse of all our heads (if taken by him);
  for having lost all goodnesse, and of late
  growne desperate mad through turbulent                           175
  passions of a distempered soule cannot
  reclayme his wickednesse, like one too farre°
  engag'd ever to returne to honestie
  againe.
MINEUS  Honestie my Lord's a stranger to him,                      180
  and mindes no more civilitie than Canniballs
  or Tartars doe, being puft up with pride
  of them vaine praises falsely given him by
  a multitude as basely minded as himselfe.
ARETAS  How they doe glorie in his bloodie deeds,                  185
  and styles him truely valiant whom the world
  reputes no better than a monster cloath'd
  in human forme.
DORA  Unheard of madnes to
  betray so many innocents, that but                               190
  for him and his damn'd shameless retinue
  had not beene executed soe.
ARETAS  How shall we
  then advise to rid us of so dangerous°
  an enemy.                                                        195
ATHENIO  Heaven will, I hope, contrive,
  his overthrow in this our expedition,
  though he securely now abides in garison
  guarded with five hundred expert Souldiers;
  thinkes Heaven nor Hell cannot molest him there,                200
  or that we dare not match within a league

[162] daseling = dazzling.
[176] reclayme [reclaim] = put right / remedy.

of his sterne countenance: such is the fopperie
of his vaine glorious humour.

MINEUS  Then name of God,°
    this night we will advance our forces where         205
    the besotted tyrant now remaines; if
    we but kill his centrie then we may more°
    boldly enter and surprise him napping
    in his bed asleepe.

ATHE NIO  That were the safest         210
    way indeed to venture on him, or preserve
    our troupes entire until our Noble Cosen
    *Abner* be arriv'd.

ARETAS  Hee's long expected.

MINEUS  But will be shortly here.         215

ATHENIO  Who, when he comes,
    comes well appointed to support this pious
    warre; our wants with his renowned fame beyond Sea.

MINEUS  Let's march directly thither; come loose no time,
    that, in necessities a wilful Crime.°       *Exeunt.* 220

        *Enter Cola like one distracted.*

COLA  Furyes and plagues torments my restles thoughts
    with gashly visions of deformed hagges,°
    infernall monsters to my thinking would
    perforce deprive me of my vitall breath.
    O that this horrid night were past away,     225
    a thousand millions for one glimpse of day.

*Cf. Macbeth*

*Flashes of fire with a horrid noise is hard; then enter Revenge with a sword in one hand*
    *and a flaming torch in the other followed by three spirits in sheets.*

    Ah, ah, th'are come againe; it thunders,
    [*Revenge knocks*] whither shall I goe hide me from the bolts
    dreadfull cracke? *Tibernus! Morton!* Why *Tibernus*,
    will none defend me from these ugly shapes?     230
    O how they presse on me; give bake, rude furyes,°

[194] i.e. be advised.
[204] i.e. in the name of God.
[207] centrie = sentry.
[220] necessities = necessity's.
[222] gashly = ghastly.

or by the hand of *Proserpine* your Queene°
I'le force you hence unto the stygian greene.°

REVENGE  I am Revenge roused from my silent cave
    by justice that revenge on thee will have,              235
    for thy base murdring of man, woman, child
    wives, widowes, nurses, virgins defiled;
    all that a tyrant could invent or doe,
    thou most inhumanly didst put them to,
    wherefore Revenge, revenge from hell is sent       240
    to leade thee to eternall punishment.

I SPIRIT  I am the soule of him, an thou wilt know,
    that in thy pistoll once didst force me blow,
    gave fire and shot me dead; hell is thy due,
    for which revenge, revenge doth thee pursue.     245

2 SPIRIT  Wee are them two poore, harmelesse country swaines,
    to get an honest living spared no paines;
    we to thy quarters went, and would from thence
    bring salt abroad just worth some eighteen pence;
    thy souldiers tooke us, stript us, shrewdly bang'd us,°    250
    then after to the gibbet and there hang'd us°
    by thy command; wherefore we doe implore
    Revenge may take revenge on thee therefore.

REVENGE  This bloodie sword and flaming torch are them
    true Emblems of thy furious strategeme,        255
    invented chiefly to depopulate
    distroy, consume, and wast the regall state°
    of this brave kingdome, or what therein's found,
    either above or underneath the ground;
    such was thy wicked malice, spleene and might    260
    for which we seeke a just revenge this night.      *Exeunt.*

COLA  This was a plot of some conjuring Papist
    to vex me with these filthy strange affrightments.
    O that I could with mighty *Jove* raine downe
    a showre of maledictions on them, cursed     265
    wretches they; the name it selfe doth vex me more
    than all them dismall shapes i've seen before.

[231] give bake = go back.

[232] Proserpina is the Roman name for Peresephone, the daughter of Zeus and Demeter who was carried off by Hades and made queen of the underworld.

[233] stygian = relating to the river Styx; gloomy, infernal.

[250] shrewdly = wickedly; bang'd [banged] = struck / beat up.

[251] gibbet = gallows.

*An Alarum. Enter Tibernus.*

What come againe, life then adieu! Now *Tibernus,*
   what makes this loud alarum?
TIBERNUS  That you may arme              270
   your selfe in hast; the rebells march into
   the towne.
COLA  He was a traitor did command
   the guard this night; goe hye thee *Tibernus,* call°
   the troupes together, crye but a *Cola, Cola,*     275
   I warrant thee they'le flie.  *Exeunt severally.*

*Alarums. Cola returns againe.*

COLA  Sa, sa, they breake
   I faith, *Cola, Cola,* crye out a *Cola!*

*One meets him and dischargeth a pistoll whereat he falls downe dead.*
*Then enter Tibernus and Souldiers.*

TIBERNUS  Sir *Carola Cola* slaine, O execrable slaughter!
   Heaven curse the rascall that was author on't;    280
   beare in the body to be embalm'd with teares,
   that when his mournefull obsequies are ended
   this Epitaph may on his tombe be engraven:
   *Angola's* glory, *Pickland's* wonder,
   *Lirenda's* terror lyes here under.    *Exeunt.*  285

*Enter Caspilona with a keeper.*

CASPILONA  Is't the counsells pleasure I shood be removed
   from hence; prethee whither?
KEEPER  Unto the Castle.
CASPILONA  'Tweare as good as I dyed as to be layd in such
   a loathsome place, where surely *Mumferret°*    290
   must be my keeper. Good friend, desire thy master
   may returne his writ; I'me sickly and not
   in case to be removed; if they conceive
   me not secure enough, or feares escape,

[257] wast = waste.
[274] hye [hie] = make haste / go quickly.

set double locks on, barre your windowes treble 295
over, any thing but departure; so
kinde each one of you have been unto me
that my imprisonment's a pleasure rather.

KEEPER  My master's willing to affoord your Lordship
all the favour lyes in him; but that, he may not. 300

CASPILONA  Why friend? 'twill be no prejudice to him,
onely his labour to informe the Court,
whom I hope are not so void of reason
but will admit a prisoner (my inferiour)
this poore request. 305

KEEPER  He dares not doe it once
the Judge and Councell's bent against you, for
'twas their expresse charge to the Sherrifes thus:
beware, your prisoner *Caspilona* hath not
more freedome given him than you may answer 310
at a thousand pound le peece.°

CASPILONA  Sayest thou so *Roger*?
Well, if there be no remedie but needs
I must depart; there's for thy dutifull
attendance. *Gives him money.* 315

KEEPER  Now heavens protect your Lordship.
[*Aside*] As I live it pitties me, this generous
noble Lord, th'are much to blame wrongs so good°
a soule.

CASPILONA  Honest *Roger*, I am disposed 320
to rest; if any kinde friend comes to visit
me, desire they would repaire another time.

KEEPER  Your will I shall observe my Lord. *Exit.*

CASPILONA  Thou art
always honest *Roger*, trustie *Roger*; 325
this is the course of fickle fortunes wheele,
last weeke reputed for a loyall subject,
now in close prison and traytor kept,
whose thoughts in that respect is full as pure
as new falne snow on mount *Libanus*; but° 330
this corrupted age declares my deerest friends

[290] Mumferret = unidentified.
[31]] le peece = a piece.
[318] th'are = they are.
[330] Mount Libanus (Lebanon): a mountain range in present-day Syria. The Bible refers to the

to be my prime accusers; well, thou God°
of justice, whose bright impartiall eye
viewes the worlds guiltie crimes, see an innocent
exposed unto a sad disastrous fate                                    335
if thy great mercy helpes me not? O then
I suffer shall with other harmeles men.

*Here he walkes in a solitary posture whilest an Angell sings.*

## THE SONG

*Cast off that drooping sadnesse Earle,*
*Be not dismaid, take heart of grace,*
*Behold a true Ellizean girle°*                                      340
*Pityes thy distressed case,*
*One that will a mortall shape,*
*Take on her for thy escape.*

CASPILONA  Some voyce my thought did whisper in mine eare,
a sweet melodious note that said: feare not                          345
thou shalt escape. Alas 'tis but my fancies
wish it had been so. No that cannot be,
for yet my soule retaines an inward joy,
the motion is divine, and makes me happy
beyond measure; bright Angell of Celestiall                          350
Paradice, to whom the safeguarde of my life
deputed is, helpe me, O helpe me to
get from this labyrinth of care; otherwise
I never shall perfect that enterprise.                    *Exit.*

beauty of its snowy peaks. See Jeremiah 18:14.
[332] well = will.
[340] Ellizean = Elysian. In Greek mythology the Elysian fields were the final resting place for the

## ACT V

*Enter Athenio, Abner and Mineus at one dore. There meets*
*them, Caspilona, Aretas and Dora at the other dore.*

CASPILONA  My Lord Generall of *Stelern*, welcome,
    welcome to *Lirenda*, thou faire son of *Mars*.
ABNER  My Lord *Caspilona*, we gratulate°
    your safe escape.
CASPILONA  Most hearty thanks.                           5
ATHENIO  Now we may boldly coape with our insulting°
    dominiering foes, whose arrogant pride
    contemn'd this nation with an infamous
    report of cowardize; base rascalls, they
    shall know we have undaunted spirits left          10
    to quell their treacherous malignant power,         ✱
    their breach of publique faith, granting quarter,
    then after, falsely murdering them.
ABNER  Is't possible
    that men who knowes the Law of Armes should be      15
    so absurd, so prophane?
CASPILONA  The universe
    cannot parallell like bloodie massakers,
    odious to God and man.
ABNER  Believe me 'twill                     20
    end shamefully; such actions cannot thrive.
ATHENIO  Ought we not deale with theirs we vanquish so?
ABNER  We scorne to imitate their baseness; what
    we doe shall be in a nobler honest way,
    true Martiall discipline.                    25
ATHENIO  Which they will ne're observe.         *A Trumpet.*
    What meanes this warning of the trumpet sound?
ARETAS  Some newes is posting hither.
ATHENIO  What tidings *Lentimos*?          *Enter Lentimos.*
LENTIMOS  Arme good, my Lord; with speed Marquis *Osirus*    30
    with a powerfull Army march hitherward,
    and hath already beene at *Motilin*,°

souls of the virtuous or heroic.
[3] gratulate = congratulate.
[6] coape [cope] =contend / fight with.
[32] Motilin = most likely refers to Timolin in County Kildare. The town was held by the Con-

where his rude, boysterous followers put
men, women, children to the sword; for certaine
'tis reported they bend their forces thence to *Fosse*.°      35
ABNER  Where they, God willing, shall have a bloodie
    banquet. Come cheerefully, my Lords, meet those
    that came so farre to seeke your manfull blowes.      *Exeunt.*

      *Enter Lysana, Tygranes, Tibernus and Souldiers. Beate a march.*

TYGRANES  Though we come short in our designe of *Fosse*,
    or must retreate from that unlukie towne,      40
    'tis not the bruite of *Abners* hasty march°
    with the whole strength of *Stelem* shoo'd make us
    stirre a foote; did his numbers equall great
    *Xerxes* army, that dranke up rivers drye,°
    the world shall testifie our willingness      45
    to meet him when and where he list.
I SOLDIER  *[Jeeringly aside]* But not
    with more hast than good speed sweet Sir,°
    I thinke we have been pretty well beaten else,
    for all good tokens; a witch, a whore, gave me°      50
    such a damnable thumpe of a stone my
    shoulders feeles the weight ont yet.
2 SOLDIER  Cursc ont for me!
    'Twas a plaguie skirmish; they fought like divells
    within; an' yee be wise not a word O fighting      55
    more.
LYSANA  We need not urge them to an open field
    for so it might prove dangerous; our men
    you see are not themselves, much weakened by
    this farre and toylesome journey.      60
TYGRANES  Wonder invades me
    you should thinke our forces lost both courage
    and experience, as if they had been
    light brained weakelings; guided by misfortune
    where no resistance could secure their lives,      65

federate forces until it was taken by Ormond (Osirus) in March 1642. Ormond reputedly offered
the surviving soldiers quarter only for them to be killed on leaving their posts.
[35] Fosse = Ross, County Wexford.
[41] bruite = rumour.
[44] Xeres was the king of Persia from 486 to 465 BC; he achieved various military victories in his
invasion of Greece.
[48] hast = haste.

     wast ever knowne they went a step to shune
     their foes? No, nor will not now, I hope, beginne
     whil'st these undaunted squadrons are reputed
     Souldiers fit to serve any Prince on earth:
     men that regards not toyle, travaile, penurie          70
     or sicknesse; nothing can divert them from
     a glorious conquest, the aime a valorous
     intention levells at.
LYSANA  I would you knew
     the proudest Monarch of the western globe         75
     hath beene as circumspect as valorous,
     least some strange accident might drowne their greatness
     in *Lethes* flowing streames; then why not we,°
     since our auspicious stars hath made our actions
     shine like theirs in equall glory; then, I pray,         80
     ought we not be as circumspect as they?
TYGRANES  You speake as if you stood in feare of them.
TIBERNUS  Come leave this different discourse; the question
     is whether Marquis *Osirus* will towards
     home, or fall on the next garisons?         85
TYGRANES  With my consent, there should not be a Castle
     left unlevell'd with the ground.
1 SOLDIER  Soft and faire,
     [*Jeeringly aside*] th'ave gotten guns and powder will make us
     smoke ifaith.         90
2 SOLDIER  Deckins take them now of late!°
     They are growne mighty valiant.
1 SOLDIER  Stout fellows!
2 SOLDIER  An I could to my granam once againe,°
     I'de ne're come looke for land in *Stelem* more.         95
1 SOLDIER  Them wood for me! I wish might die a pander.°
2 SOLDIER  And with lesse wit than either goose or gander.

*Enter Osirus.*

OSIRUS  What serious conference is this betweene
     you gentlemen; are you growne faint of late?

[50] token = omen / portent.
[78] In Greek myth the Lethe was a river in Hades, the water of which produced forgetfulness in those who drank it.
[91] Deckins [dickens] = the devil.
[94] granam = grandmother.

See the multitude of your encreasing foes,                                    100
how earnest they like venom'd spiders hast°
to take us in a tangled web of woe,
and here you stand aloofe, like men dismaid,
as if it nought concern'd to heare or see
the subject of *Lirendas Tragedie*.                                           105
TYGRANES  Wee onely waite your honors chiefe command.
OSIRUS  For shame, speed to your severall troopes; let not
your warme blood freeze in them active veines whilst
such a noble blest occasions offer'd.
Come then couragiously, and the day's yours              110
in spight of hell and all malignant powers.              *Exeunt.*

    *Soone after th' Alarums begun, enter Lysana, his weapon drawne.*

LYSANA  All, all's lost; our troupes are broken basely.
O that I had a paire of *Dedalus* wings,°
or mounted on swift *Pegassus* to passe°
from hence invisible; my thoughts foretold                                    115
this heavy dismall day; I would begon,°
but that I know not whither and want a guide:
a guide, a guide, a thousand pound for a guide!°
Feare makes them deafe; they cannot heare the golden
offers of great *Lestrell's* sonne; well then, I will°                        120
proclaime it once again: five thousand pound,
ten thousand for a guide, my whole estate
to him will be my guide!                                *Exit.*

    *Osirus and Abner meet severally, weapons drawne. Alarums.*

ABNER  *Vive le Roy!* Advance, th'artillery is ours.
OSIRUS  Not so fast bold Traytor, stand!                                      125
ABNER  Traytor Sir,
as loyall to my Soveraigne as they selfe,
and to thy face I vouch it now, proud Marquis.

---

[96] Them wood for me = I agree [?]; pander = pimp / procurer.
[101] hast = haste.
[113] In Greek mythology Daedalus was the legendary Athenian craftsman who built two pairs of
wings out of wax and feathers so he and his son Icarus could escape the imprisonment of king
Minos. However Icarus ignored his father's warning not to fly too near the sun and the wax
melted, causing him to fall into the sea and was drowned.
[114] Pegasus was a winged horse in Greek mythology.
[116] begon = be gone.
[118] Cf. Shakespeare, *Richard III*, V. 4. 7.

*They fight. Abner closes within him.*

ABNER Yeeld sir yeeld, you are my lawfull prisoner.
OSIRUS Thine? Let him perish yeelds to any of                    130
    thy faction.

*Enter Tygranes. Alarums.*

TYGRANES Rescue! The generall's in danger.

*Here Tygranes renewes the fight. Dora steps in, and knocks downe Tygranes. Tibernus*
*to his rescue, where after a short skirmish they retire fighting severally. Exeunt.*

*Enter Abner, Athenio, Mineus, Caspilona and Dora.*

ABNER They cannot boast our reputations blemisht
    in the losse of this late victorie, so
    faire lye ours. No, the chance of war's uncertaine,           135
    and no man ought to grudge at what is past,
    since them we did encounter last are fled,
    loaden with the luggage of your heavy blowes
    and glad to scape so too; but least some carping
    *Momu's* falsely might attribute to our actions°            140
    what destinie brings on the stoutest he°
    that lives, were not the gods constrain'd to hide
    themselves in hollow caves of Egypt, when
    fierce *Typheus* did pursue their deityes,°
    and mighty *Cesar*, too glad to flye                        145
    from stout Lord *Nennius* in the Brittans warre,°
    then wounded with his owne infected weapon?
    How many like examples could I mention
    of powerfull armyes overthrowne by fate?

[120] Lestrell most likely refers to the earl of Leicester, father to Lord Lisle (i.e. Lysana).
[141] Momu = a person who habitually finds fault (from Momus, the Greek god of censure and ridicule.)
[142] he = man.
[145] Typheus (also known as Typhon) was a monstrous giant of Greek myth who became associated in the writings of Herodotus with the evil Egyptian deity Set.
[147–8] According to Geoffrey Monmouth's *History of the kings of Britain* (c.1136) Nennius was a prince of Britain during the time of Julius Caesar's invasions. The two fought in single combat. Caesar struck Nennius on the head, but his sword became embedded in his opponent's shield. After they separated Nennius continued fighting and used Caesar's sword to kill several Romans.

Witnes *Xeres*, *Hannibal*, *Darius*, the                                        150
Grecian Troupes at *Troy*, Troyans themselves,
Emperors, Kings, Princes, Dukes, men whose
aspiring thoughts mounted above the clouds,
yet were brought low and raised againe as wavering
fortune went; which best becomes a Souldier,                                     155
and proves him truely valiant that will sleight
the frowning chekes of proud *Bellona's* height;
since nothing can be more commendable
than an undaunted generous spirit
(the square true warlike vertues measured by).°                                  160
I dare assure the meanest of this nation
will maintaine it, that posteritie may have
a patterne fit for them to imitate.
Briefly, let's bravely forward that we may
regaine more than is lost another day.                        *Exeunt.*  165

*Enter the Souldiers merrily disposed, singing the following Song.*

1 SOLDIER  *In dayes of yore, not long before*
  *The last warres here were ended,*
  *With maid and Wife, a Souldiers life*
  *Was most of all commended.*
2 SOLDIER  *For why they fought, not then for nought,*                            170
  *Not one among thrice twentie,*
  *But had good drinke, with store of chinke,*°
  *Their pockets seldome emptie.*
1 SOLDIER  *But now adayes, that joviall prayse*
  *Is turned topsie turvie,*                                                      175
  *To sweate, to dirt, to a louzie shirt,*
  *To scratching itch, or scurvie.*
2 SOLDIER  *Nay one more thing, doth grieve us sore,*
  *Weyes me that I can say,*
  *Sir reverence, without offence,*                                              180
  *Tis call'd the Captains pay.*
1 SOLDIER  *Which Lord forbid, if our foes did*
  *Crave vengeance come with quicknes,*
  *They never could, no if they would,*
  *Wish a more hellish sicknes.*                                                 185

He died fifteen days later of his head wound.
[161] square = example / standard.

2 SOLDIER  *If pillage wood doe us some good,*
    *Commanders are the boulder,*
    *That plundring* Dicke *hath taught the tricke,°*
    *You must not this good Souldier.*

1 SOLDIER  *Thus we are serv'd, and almost sterv'd,°*        190
    *'Twixt one disease or other,*
    *The best of us can well sing thus,*
    *Shake hands with me kinde brother.*
    Hang melancholly, a pound of sorrow
    will not pay an ounce of debt, so mad cap so!      195
    [*Claps him in on the shoulder.*]

2 SOLDIER  Zlid, I have sown all my wild oates already!

1 SOLDIER  *Wild as a bucke, or tame as a ducke,*
    *Or sillier than a coxcombe,*
    *No land, no wealth, no thanks, no health,*
    *And is't not therefore all's one?*      200

2 SOLDIER  This riming humour likes me well.    *Enter another Souldier.*

3 SOLDIER  Newes, newes!

2 SOLDIER  And what's thy newes good-man foole?

3 SOLDIER  Brave newes.
    Our generall, Sir *Vavasiro.*      205

2 SOLDIER  And what of him?

3 SOLDIER  Sayes we shall have old cutting throats anon,
    and pillage boyes, pillage till yee sweat againe.

1 SOLDIER  The Castle is not yeelded yet?

3 SOLDIER  Within an houre      210
    it will at farthest; where if we doe not
    dance attendance quickly, others will play
    at sweepe stakes all.

1 SOLDIER  Very true, an honest lad.

2 SOLDIER  A very, very arrant —— honest lad.    *Exeunt.*  215

*A short Alarum. Enter Souldiers dragging in men and women whom they kill, then fall*
      *off. Enter Caspilona, Dora and Lentimos.*

CASPILONA  You see this dolefull object, gentlemen,
    and perceive what need our friends have of some
    swift assistance, that peradventure might°

[173] chinke [chink] = coins / ready money.
[188] Obscure. Dick could be a generic name for an officer.
[191] sterv'd = starved.

redeeme more than is held expedient;
we are not therefore come to loose time in                    220
a tedious consultation; seeing
your worth and valours knowne already,
then, name of God, charge home, lets hast away,°
Heaven will assuredly grant this our day.              *Exeunt.*

   *Alarums with Drum and Trumpet. Enter Vavasiro pursued by Caspilona.*

CASPILONA  Wee thought Angolean sparkes could not tell how°     225
   to run before; proud *Vavasiro* dyes.
VAVASIRO  O spare my life victorious *Caspilona*,
   and I will faithfull submit thy contrite
   prisoner.
CASPILONA  That but immediately didst butcher°                 230
   those without remorse or pity; goe learne
   to be a penitent, and know we use
   mercy to them doth ours more oft abuse.    *He leads him off a prisoner.*

   *Enter Athenio, Mineus, Aretas and Dora.*

ATHENIO  Now he perceives his mischievous intention°
   will not take, makes him the more adventurous,            235
   or rather desperate, that no advice
   (from his best friends) can persuade him once to
   slake what lyes in him to execute, though
   it sinke him deeper than the worst of evils;
   or that he may be disappointed, yet                      240
   will not seeme to know it, so farre a bloody
   passion doth transport him that he reflects
   on nothing but revenge; whom to surprise°
   or murder (though innocent) he makes no
   scruple on't more than *Cola* did before he fell          245
   under the waight of his owne vices.
MINEUS  A Tyger
   truly by name and nature, a slave too,
   that torments himselfe worse then he can doe us,

[219] peradventure = by chance, perhaps.
[223] hast = haste.
[226] sparkes [spark] = a depreciatory term for a foppish, affected man.
[230] That but = You who.
[234] he = Tygranes.

how good a face soever he puts on,                                     250
or that rude multitude doth follow him;
we are become their betters in the field,
heaven favouring us with good successe, that
now their malice shewes not halfe the violence
that hitherto it did, though no good will                              255
be wanting to effect it if they could.°
Wherefore 'tis certaine then: he that will steere
blacke envies barke in a warme Sea of blood°
must justly perish in that fatall flood.

ARETAS  To witness this let me present unto                            260
your memory a few in *Stelern* only,
that like a torrent of impetuous furie
went raging downe the steep descent of death,
and lost themselves therein: *Albinus, Celar,*
*Daretas, Philanax* with their *Rabi*,                                 265
ringleader Sir *Carola Cola* (for whose
deere sake they yet lament, whereby 'tis palpable,
heaven grieves at our reproach.)

DORA  We could rehearse
as many more sufficient to amaze                                       270
the most obdurate *Round-head* of them all;
but to expresse that we regard *Tygranes*
forces lesse than may be spoken of whilest
we can wield these armes, such cutting weapons
that can soone decide the best of eithers right.                       275

*Enter Lentimos.*

MINEUS  Behold *Lentimos*, with some sad newes it's fear'd.

ATHENIO  It shall not worke in us, the worst may follow.
    Now Cuze, how goes squares abroade?°

LENTIMOS  That Lord *Tygranes*
with his army doth commit all kinde of                                 280
cruelties, and march directly hither.

ATHENIO  What strength can you discover him to be?

LENTIMOS  About five thousand, horse and foote.

ATHENIO  Were he ten thousand strong it matters not;
    wee'll expect him at *Lesterne* passage. Goe                       285

[244] surprise = attack / assail suddenly.
[256–7] i.e. they do not lack the will / inclination to affect it [i.e. violence] if they could ...
[259] barke = a small boat.

take a hundred musqueteers along with you,
and make it good before his van arrives;
wee'll follow after in all convenient              *Exit Lentimos.*
speed. Wee are not ignorant, noble kinsmen,
how insolent, bold and audacious                     290
these folorne wretches doe contest with us
for what's our birth-right and inheritance;
that in defence of that, or what is deerest
to us, wee are to expose ourselves to death.
The wrong done our poore, harmeles people, all      295
the most studied torments was inflicted
on them for which wee chiefly move, attired
in armes to rouze their stupid conscience that
will strictly answer for't; whil'st now each goodness
doth forsake them it cannot passe so currant        300
but wee may give an end to their vaine hopes,
heaven yielding us that priviledge, though not
worthy yet wee need not doubt it. Then let us
arme, as well interiour as exteriourly,
to be in a fit posture 'gainst he comes.               305
Let trumpets sound, strike up our Martiall drums.

     *Drums and Trumpets as they depart. Enter Tygranes and Tibernus.*

TYGRANES  Where lyes their Campe?
TIBERNUS  At *Lestern* passage, some three
   miles distant hence.
TYGRANES  Are they strongly fortified?           310
TIBERNUS  Impregnable,
   and hardly can be forc'd without great losse
   of ours.
TYGRANES  Have they artillery thinke you?
TIBERNUS  Yes, some small piece they have.      315
TYGRANES  Which shall be mine
   or mine theirs ere bright *Titans* rayes decline.
   Goe, bid the officers be readie for
   intend to march against them presently.°     *Exit Tibernus.*
   A Curse on his life for me that will not breake     320
   on them, or use the most extremitie he
   can devise, a storme of tortures, until

[279] squares = matters / events.

the mountaine of their vicious will
are brought to nothing. O that it lay within
my power to cut off roote and branch together;          325
if not, besure, I'le doe my best endeavour.            *Exit.*

*Soone after the Alarums begun, hee returnes with his weapon drawne.*

TYGRANES  All will not doe, some horrible wicked
    destinie befriends them; our men drop downe
    on every side, whereat they seeme to scoffe
    and floute, not giving ground an inch. Well,          330
    well, *Tygranes* shall not be affronted thus;
    I'le sooner die, and fight it out to the
    last man; death shall not hold me.°

*Enter Tibernus.*

TIBERNUS  Remove your standing Sir,
    I doe beseech you Sir withdraw your person          335
    to some other place, for hence I can descrie
    a piece right levell'd to give fire at you.
TYGRANES  That man is curst in his mothers wombe will
    shun a Canon shot. [*A shot is given forth*] ah, I am wounded, wounded
    beyond recovery! Now, O now I feele          340
    the painefull seizures of untimely death
    on the remainder of my vitall breath.
    Vaine world adieu, farewell brave Souldiers all;
    be not dismaid at Lord *Tygrane's* fall.
TIBERNUS  Heaven's blessed messenger, receive thy soule.          345

*Souldiers step in.*

1 SOLDIER  But is he dead indeed?
TIBERNUS  As cold as stone.
1 SOLDIER  Wee that have loved him when he lived, and found
    his open heart a Magazine of bountie
    must (if nature be not too ungratefull)          350
    shed brinish teares.
TIBERNUS  That were effeminate,
    and indiscretion too. Now hee's lost; if in

[318] i.e. we intend.

the view of our adversaries we seeme
to grieve it may occasion greater evils,     355
having th'advantage of our generall losse;
then silence best becomes you for the present;
all that is requisite must be to beare
his bodie hence unto his tent. So sadly on,
that when true sorrow's in the hearts of all,     360
his Corps may have a noble funeral.     *Exeunt.*

*Beat a march. Enter Abner, Athenio, Mineus, Aretas, Dora and Lentimos.*

ATHENIO  Thus through the help and furtherance of heaven
    our most malignant enemy's overcome;
    glad to play least in sight went sneking home,°
    who not long since, for oaths and threatnings, might     365
    terrifie the gods, or subdue the world;
    that neither Heaven nor Hell was thought on once,
    or what was spoken of them were but fictions
    which lead them to the gulfe of desperation.
ABNER  We must pursue this blessed victorie,     370
    making our withered hopes bud forth in blossomes
    of never fading honour.
DORA  It adds unto
    our comfort, Noble friends, that *Caspilona*
    goes bravely to.     375
ABNER  Yes, and God willing
    we intend so to until we purge the
    Kingdome of these drones, them viperous Locusts.
    Come, follow me.
LENTIMOS  But stay my Lord, here comes     380
    a Post with letters to your Lordship.     *Enter a Post with letters.*
ABNER  How letters? Let me see.
    Had they defer'd it but one fortnight longer!
ATHENIO  What newes doe them import?
ABNER  A proclomation     385
    for one whole twelve moneth and a day's Cessation.
LENTIMOS  This works in us a greater admiration,
    that being in the full height of our conquest
    as prosperous as might be expected,
    brave *Abner's* shining virtues like the Sun     390

[333] hold = stop.

out of a new *Horizon*, all the graces
delightfull Mars could give or we deserve,
must through his needles fond cessation rest°
on the drowsie Couch of darke Oblivion;
it is a pill few Souldiers can digest.                                    395
ATHENIO  Which best approves our loyaltie.
ABNER  But you
and we must yeeld obedience to it,
though not so well contented; howsoever
your forces must unto their garrisons,                                   400
and if our wrongs be not repaired thereby
we will againe renew this Tragedie.                      *Exeunt.*

> *Solemne Musick's heard whil'st an Angell appears to perclose the Scaene*
> *with this following Song.*

> *Peace to this bright resplendent spheare,*
> *Blessings numberless be there,*
> *Endles joyes that doth abide,*                                         405
> *In Elizeum too, beside,*
> *Nothing present may defile*
> *This victorious sacred Ile.*
> *Come yee Gods and Goddesses,*
> *That affecteth Peacefull blisse,*                                      410
> *Helpe Victoria to disperse,*
> *Each blessing on this universe,*
> *That dissentions broyles and jarres,*
> *May end with these uncivill warres.*
> *Haste, O haste delightfull Queene,*                                    415
> *With your Laurells fresh and greene,*
> *Grace this nation with a Crowne,*
> *Of perpetuall renowne,*
> *Since their warlike merits are,*
> *Past the limits of Compare.*                                          420

> *Musicke as the Angel vanisheth.*

[364] Obscure.
[394] needles = needless; fond = desirous of / inclined towards. Mars, the god of war, is desirous
of this 'needles' cessation …

## THE EPILOGUE

Least any worthy here misliks this play,
Our Author for himselfe desired me say,
That wilfull error made him not ascend
PARNASSUS or mount IDA to offend[1]
Or give the least distast: his thoughts are free,
And void of such a grosse impuritie.
Desire of your contentment was the cause,
If he did violate the Muses Lawes;
But such a noble, worthy Audience
In their grave judgments will I hope dispence                    10
With such, if any be; since true affection
Submitts before it traverse a correction.
All wee request then, as the case thus stands,
In token you are pleased, doe but clap hands.


*Laus Deo, Virginia Maria.*

---

1  Mount Parnassus in central Greece is associated with Apollo and the Muses and was regarded
   as the source of poetic inspiration. Mount Ida in Crete was the reputed birthplace of the Greek
   god Zeus.

# Appendix: Identifying the characters in history

All the principal characters of *Cola's furie* have either allegorical or anagrammatical names which half-disguise and half-reveal actual historical personages. Bentley's 1956 comment that 'a little study of the play and of the Rebellion of 1641 would probably enable one to identify most of the characters' (Bentley, 95) is somewhat optimistic: it takes rather more than 'a little' study. Some earlier commentators focused mainly on attempting such identifications: in this appendix I list these, up to and including G.C. Duggan.[1]

## (A) ON THE ANGOLEAN (ENGLISH) SIDE

*Pitho* = Sir William Parsons, and *Berosus* = Sir John Borlase, the draconian lords justices at the outbreak of the rebellion, both New English planters who quickly emerged as Parliament-men.[2]

*Osirus* = the Earl of Ormond, leading royalist in Ireland, later viceroy.

*Cola* = Sir Charles Coote the elder, rapacious New English colonist, notorious among Catholics for atrocities committed in the wars, both in Wicklow and in various places near Dublin. Shot mysteriously, perhaps by one of his own men, at Trim in May 1642 (iv, 277–85).

*Lysana* = Lord Lisle, commander of cavalry and Ormond's second-in-command, who fled ignominiously at the battle of Poulmounty, outside New Ross, in March 1643 (v, 112–23): the scene shows him desperately calling for a guide to escape, in a manner strongly reminiscent of Shakespeare's *Richard III*.

*Crambich* = Colonel Crawford, one of the commanders of Munro's Scottish Presbyterian troops in Ulster; Munro himself is probably represented as *Sir Daretas,* although the suggestion that Daretas has been killed by the end of the play (v, 260–6) casts doubt on this identification (Munro did not die until 1675).

## ON THE LIRENDEAN (IRISH) SIDE

*Cephalon* = Patrick Barnewall of Kilbrew, the Pale gentleman in his sixties who was racked on the orders of Parsons and Borlase in the aftermath of the rebel-

---

1  These include hints from the scarcely decipherable annotations already mentioned.

2  I have gathered the information in these notes largely from the following sources: John T. Gilbert (ed.), *History of the Confederacy and the war in Ireland, 1641–1653*, 7 vols (Dublin, 1882–91), which prints Bellings' account as well as many contemporary documents, and also the *Aphorismical discovery* (see above, n. 15 in my introduction to this edition) and C. Meehan, *The Confederation of Kilkenny* (Dublin, 1873). There is a still-useful summary account of the fighting in Lowe, 'Some aspects of the wars', see n. 4 of my introduction above.

lion, in spring 1642 (iii, 103–32).[3] The play, however, consolidates both its dramatic and ideological effects by showing Cola (Coote) supervising the racking
in person.

*Rufus* = Sir John Read (Latin 'rufus', meaning 'red', perhaps involving a
pun), a Catholic of Scots birth, sent to Dublin as an agent of the confederates to
request clemency early in 1642, and also racked in an attempt to get an admis-
sion of royal complicity in the rebellion (iii, 134–51).

*Abner* = Sir Thomas Preston, commander-in-chief of the confederate army.

*Theodorike* = Owen Roe O'Neill, finest of the generals and leader of the Old
Irish faction.

*Guyrua* = Maguire, Ulster chieftain in 1641.

More tentatively, G.C. Duggan further identified the following:

*Mineus* = Lord Mountgarret, and *Athenio* = Lord Antrim, both important
leaders of the confederates' Assembly and Council.

*Dora* = Patrick Darcy, the confederation's lawyer.

*Caspilona* = Lord Castlehaven. (Bentley reads the relevant faint BL MS anno-
tation as '-ldlae': this may possibly represent a Latin version of 'Audley', which
was James Touchet's title before he was created earl of Castlehaven.) Visiting
Dublin to try to intercede on the confederates' behalf, Castlehaven was impris-
oned but escaped, in disguise, in September 1642. In the play he bribes a keeper
to turn a blind eye, and is assisted by a Lirendean gentlewoman (iv, 286–337).

*Tygranes* = Murrough, Lord Inchiquin, hereditary chief of the O'Briens of
Thomond, nevertheless fighting against the confederates. One of the causes of
Inchiquin's notoriety, apart from his repeated changes of religion and allegiance,
was his brutal and ruthless method of warfare (giving rise to his well-known Irish
nickname *Murchadh na dTóiteán* or Murrough of the Burnings).

I would modify these suggestions as follows. I disagree that Tygranes is
Inchiquin, and suggest rather that he is Lord Moore of Mellifont, who was in
fact spectacularly shot to pieces by Owen Roe O'Neill's gunner at the battle of
Portlester (in September 1643, immediately before the cessation). In the play,
Tygranes is killed by a cannon shot at long distance, while, as indeed Duggan
remarks, Inchiquin lived on and throve. It is also possible that the other
Angolean commander Tibernus, about whom Bentley and Duggan are silent,
may be identified with Sir Henry Tichborne who was appointed as Lord Justice
in place of the dismissed Parsons in April 1643. This identification, however,
would present a difficulty, in that it represents a serious distortion of the facts.

---

3   I thank Dr Bríd McGrath for useful discussion of the historical personnel represented as char-
    acters in the play, based on her research in 'A biographical dictionary of the Irish House of
    Commons, 1640–1641' (unpublished TCD PhD thesis, 1998).

Tichborne had refused to carry out summary executions on prisoners taken at the skirmish at Rathconnell after quarter had been given (earlier that spring). If Tibernus does indeed represent Tichborne, Burkhead would be tarring him with the same brush as Parsons, who actually ordered the killings.[4] When, in the play, four soldiers enter and say: 'they call for quarter, and will yield the Castle / if we grant it them', Tibernus instructs them to promise quarter falsely and a massacre follows, starkly rendered by the stage-direction 'Men, women and children enter and are killed'. This distortion would be a lapse from the play's fidelity to events, which is one of its greatest strengths. One's general conclusion from a matching of historical fact to dramatic representation is that Burkhead is not generally careless with fact, and indeed this accuracy is felt as an imperative and essential part of the project of the play. As against this, and in the category of positive rather than negative distortion, there does seem to be a rather startling piece of wishful thinking at v, 129 – of a piece with the aggrandisement of Preston noted earlier – when Abner is represented as taking Osirus (Ormond) prisoner.

Burkhead omits the character of Vavasiro from the *dramatis personae* even though he appears briefly in the final act. Vavasiro can be confidently identified as Sir Charles Vavasour, head of the Munster regiment, who was defeated and taken prisoner by Castlehaven (Caspilona) at Cloughleigh in June 1643. The manner in which he is shown mercy by Caspilona mirrors Castlehaven's description of the event in his *Memoirs*.[5]

Patricia Coughlan

---

4  See C. Meehan, *Confederation*, pp 65–81.
5  See *The memoirs of James, Lord Audley, earl of Castlehaven, his engagement and carriage in the wars of Ireland from the year 1642 to the year 1651* (London, 1680), pp 32–4.